Air Fryer Cookbook for Beginners

Simple, Tasty, Crispy, and Healthy Air Fryer Recipes for All Occasions: A Beginner's Guide to Cooking the British Way

By

Connor Elliott

Table of contents

INTRODUCTION

Welcome to the "Air Fryer Cookbook for Beginners: UK Edition"!

ABOUT THIS COOKBOOK

This cookbook has been specifically crafted for beginners in the United Kingdom who are looking to embark on an exciting culinary journey with the help of an air fryer. Whether you're new to the world of air frying or a seasoned cook, this cookbook is designed to be your go-to resource for simple, delicious, and healthier recipes that cater to the unique tastes and preferences of the UK.

Inside these pages, you'll find a treasure trove of air-fried creations, ranging from classic British comfort foods to international delights. We've carefully selected and crafted recipes to help you explore the versatility and convenience of air frying. Whether you're craving crispy fish and chips, flavourful vegetarian dishes, or delectable desserts, we've got you covered.

BENEFITS OF COOKING WITH AN AIR FRYER

Air frying is a game-changer in the world of home cooking. This innovative kitchen appliance offers a multitude of benefits, especially for those looking to enjoy great-tasting food with fewer calories and less oil. Here are some of the key advantages:

Healthier Eating: Air frying uses hot air circulation to cook food, requiring minimal to no oil, which reduces the overall fat content in your meals. This is perfect for anyone aiming to maintain a balanced diet.

Crispy and Delicious Results: Despite using less oil, air fryers can achieve that desirable crispy texture on your favourite dishes. Imagine indulging in the crunch of fried food without the guilt.

Faster Cooking Times: Air fryers are known for their speed. They can cook food faster than traditional methods, making them ideal for busy individuals and families.

Easy Clean-up: With no messy splatters and minimal oil to contend with, cleaning up after cooking is a breeze.

Versatility: You can air fry a wide range of dishes, from appetizers to main courses, and even desserts. The possibilities are nearly endless.

TIPS FOR GETTING STARTED

Before you dive into the recipes in this cookbook, it's essential to get acquainted with your air fryer and some fundamental tips to ensure successful air frying experiences:

Read Your Air Fryer Manual: Familiarize yourself with the user manual that came with your air fryer. This will provide specific guidelines and safety instructions for your particular appliance.

Preheat Your Air Fryer: Just like an oven, preheating your air fryer helps ensure even cooking and better results. Most recipes in this cookbook will specify whether preheating is required.

Use the Right Cookware: Ensure that you use cookware suitable for air frying, such as baskets, racks, and pans that are compatible with your air fryer. Non-stick accessories are often the best choice.

Monitor Your Food: Keep an eye on your food during the cooking process, and follow the suggested flip and shake instructions in the recipes to ensure even cooking.

Experiment and Have Fun: Don't be afraid to experiment with the recipes and make them your own. The more you use your air fryer, the better you'll become at customizing dishes to your taste.

Now that you're armed with an understanding of what this cookbook offers, the benefits of air frying, and some essential tips, it's time to embark on your air frying adventure. Get ready to enjoy delicious and wholesome meals while discovering the joy of cooking with your air fryer. Happy cooking!

CHAPTER 1: GETTING TO KNOW YOUR AIR FRYER

In this chapter, we will delve into the essential aspects of your air fryer. Understanding the types of air fryers, their parts and components, and how to maintain and clean your appliance will set the foundation for successful air frying experiences.

TYPES OF AIR FRYERS

Air fryers come in various types and sizes to cater to different needs. In the UK, you'll commonly find the following:

Basket-Style Air Fryers: These air fryers feature a pull-out basket where you place your food. They are known for their simplicity and ease of use. Basket-style air fryers are available in different sizes, making them suitable for individuals, couples, or families.

Oven-Style Air Fryers: Resembling small convection ovens, these air fryers have a flat cooking surface and allow you to air fry larger quantities of food at once. They often come with multiple racks, providing versatility for cooking different items simultaneously.

Toaster Oven and Air Fryer Combos: Some appliances combine the functions of a toaster oven and an air fryer, giving you the option to toast, bake, roast, and air fry all in one. These are great for kitchens with limited space.

Digital vs. Manual Air Fryers: Air fryers come in both digital and manual control options. Digital models offer precise temperature and timing settings, while manual ones provide simplicity and ease of use.

Before proceeding, it's important to check the user manual that came with your air fryer to understand its specific features and functions.

PARTS AND COMPONENTS

To make the most of your air fryer, it's essential to familiarize yourself with its components. The following are typical parts found in an air fryer:

Basket or Cooking Pan: This is where you place your food for cooking. It may have a perforated bottom for air circulation.

Basket Release Button: Used to detach the cooking basket from the main unit for cleaning or food transfer.

Control Panel: This interface allows you to set temperature, cooking time, and select cooking modes.

Heating Element: The heating element is responsible for heating the air inside the fryer.

Fan: The fan circulates hot air within the appliance, ensuring even cooking.

Cooling System: Located at the back or sides of the appliance, the cooling system prevents it from overheating during use.

Drip Tray: This removable tray catches any grease or oil that may drip from your food, making clean-up easier.

Racks and Skewers: Some air fryers come with additional accessories like racks and skewers, allowing you to cook multiple items or skewered foods simultaneously.

Understanding these components will help you assemble, use, and maintain your air fryer correctly.

MAINTENANCE AND CLEANING

Proper maintenance and cleaning of your air fryer are vital to ensure its longevity and safe operation. Here are some key tips:

Unplug and Cool Down: Always unplug your air fryer and allow it to cool down before cleaning.

Remove and Clean the Basket: After each use, remove the cooking basket and wash it with warm, soapy water or place it in the dishwasher if it's dishwasher-safe.

Clean the Interior: Wipe down the interior with a damp cloth or sponge. If there is stubborn residue, use a non-abrasive sponge or brush.

Check the Heating Element: Regularly inspect the heating element for any food particles or residue. If you notice build-up, consult your user manual for guidance on cleaning.

Empty the Drip Tray: Dispose of any accumulated grease or oil from the drip tray and clean it thoroughly.

Exterior Cleaning: Wipe down the exterior of the air fryer to remove any grease or fingerprints.

Understanding the types, components, and proper maintenance of your air fryer will set you on the right path for successful air frying adventures. In the upcoming chapters, you'll put this knowledge to good use as you prepare delicious dishes tailored to the UK palate.

CHAPTER 2: ESSENTIAL COOKING TECHNIQUES

In this chapter, we will delve into the fundamental cooking techniques required to create delicious air-fried dishes. Mastering these techniques is key to achieving the best results in your air fryer.

PREHEATING YOUR AIR FRYER

Just like traditional ovens, it's often recommended to preheat your air fryer. Preheating ensures that your air fryer reaches the desired cooking temperature before you place your food inside. This is especially important for achieving even and consistent results. To preheat your air fryer:

Turn it On: Plug in your air fryer and set it to the desired temperature as specified in your recipe. Preheating usually takes 3-5 minutes.

Let It Warm Up: Allow your air fryer to run until it reaches the pre-set temperature. Most air fryers will indicate when they're ready.

Preheat Time Considerations: Not all recipes require preheating, so always refer to the specific instructions in your recipe. Some air fryers may also have a preheat setting.

UNDERSTANDING TEMPERATURE AND TIMING

Temperature and timing are two critical factors in air frying. Different foods require different cooking temperatures and times. Here are some general guidelines:

Temperature Control: Most air fryers allow you to set the cooking temperature anywhere between 100°C to 200°C (212°F to 392°F). Lower temperatures are ideal for dehydrating or reheating, while higher temperatures are perfect for crisping and browning.

Timing: Cooking times can vary widely depending on the type and quantity of food. It's essential to follow the recommended times in your recipes and check for doneness as you become more familiar with your air fryer. Start by following the recipe instructions, and adjust as needed.

Temperature and Time Adjustments: If you find that your food is browning too quickly on the outside but still raw on the inside, lower the cooking temperature and extend the cooking time. Conversely, if your food isn't browning enough, increase the temperature or extend the cooking time.

FLIPPING AND SHAKING

Flipping and shaking are crucial steps in ensuring even cooking and crispy results. Here's how to do it:

Flipping: For foods like chicken wings, patties, or fries, flip them halfway through the cooking time to ensure both sides get equally crispy. Use tongs or a spatula to turn the items gently.

Shaking: Some air fryers have a shaking reminder or a specific pause button to remind you to shake the basket. Shaking redistributes the food and promotes even browning. If your air fryer doesn't have this feature, manually pull out the basket and shake it gently during the cooking process.

USING OIL AND COOKING SPRAY

Air frying is known for its ability to create crispy food with minimal oil, but a little oil or cooking spray can enhance the results. Here's how to use them effectively:

Spray or Brush: Use a cooking spray or a brush to apply a thin, even layer of oil to the food. This is particularly helpful when air frying items like vegetables, ensuring they crisp up nicely.

Choose the Right Oil: opt for oils with a high smoke point, such as vegetable oil, canola oil, or grape seed oil. These oils can withstand the high cooking temperatures of the air fryer without producing smoke or an unpleasant taste.

Be Mindful of Quantities: Use oil sparingly. You'll find that a little goes a long way in an air fryer. Too much oil can result in greasy food and smoke.

Mastering these essential cooking techniques will give you the confidence to tackle a wide range of air fryer recipes. In the following chapters, you'll put these skills to use as you explore a variety of delectable dishes tailor-made for the UK palate.

CHAPTER 3: SAFETY TIPS AND GUIDELINES

Safety is of paramount importance when using any kitchen appliance, including your air fryer. In this chapter, we will explore the key safety considerations to ensure your air frying experiences are enjoyable and risk-free.

PROPER PLACEMENT AND VENTILATION

Location Matters: Place your air fryer on a stable, heat-resistant surface in a well-ventilated area. Ensure that there's enough space around the appliance for proper airflow, as this helps prevent overheating.

Avoid Overhead Cabinets: Don't place your air fryer under overhead cabinets or in enclosed spaces, as this can trap heat and affect its performance. Provide at least 4-6 inches of clearance above the appliance.

Keep It Level: Make sure your air fryer is on a level surface to prevent any accidental tipping.

Check the Cord: Ensure that the power cord is not hanging over the edge of the counter to prevent tripping hazards.

Be Mindful of Heat: The exterior of the air fryer can get hot during operation. Avoid touching it, and use oven mitts or a kitchen towel when handling the appliance.

COOKWARE AND UTENSIL RECOMMENDATIONS

Air Fryer-Safe Cookware: Use cookware and utensils that are specifically designed for air frying. Most air fryers come with accessories like cooking baskets and racks. Stick to these or ones recommended in your user manual.

Non-Stick Accessories: Non-stick surfaces make cleaning easier and reduce the chances of food sticking to the cooking basket or tray. Ensure that you follow the manufacturer's guidelines for care and maintenance of non-stick components.

Avoid Metal Utensils: Refrain from using metal utensils that could scratch or damage the non-stick coating on the cooking basket. opt for silicone, wood, or plastic utensils.

Avoid Glass and Ceramic: Avoid using glass or ceramic cookware in your air fryer, as the sudden temperature changes can cause them to shatter.

COMMON SAFETY CONCERNS

Watch for Smoke: If you notice excessive smoke coming from your air fryer, immediately turn it off, unplug it, and let it cool down. This could indicate a problem, such as an oil spill or a malfunction.

Avoid Overfilling: Do not overfill the cooking basket or tray with food. Overcrowding can obstruct air circulation and result in uneven cooking.

Don't Block Ventilation: Ensure that the air vents on your air fryer remain unobstructed during operation. Blocking these vents can lead to overheating.

Be Cautious with Grease: Be careful when handling hot, greasy items. Use the appropriate utensils and allow items to cool slightly before serving.

Supervise Children: Keep children away from the air fryer during operation. The exterior can get hot, and the appliance should not be accessible to unsupervised children.

Use on a Flat Surface: Always place your air fryer on a stable, flat surface to prevent accidents and ensure proper operation.

Clean Regularly: Regularly clean the cooking basket, drip tray, and other components to prevent the build-up of grease and food particles, which can be a fire hazard.

By following these safety tips and guidelines, you can enjoy the convenience of air frying while minimizing risks and ensuring a safe cooking environment. In the upcoming chapters, you'll apply these safety principles as you create delicious air-fried dishes.

CHAPTER 4: AIR FRYING BASICS

In this chapter, we'll explore the fundamentals of air frying by diving into some beloved classics: Crispy Air-Fried Foods, Perfectly Roasted Vegetables, and Golden-Brown Fries and Chips. Each recipe comes with cooking time, servings, ingredients, instructions, and nutritional information in UK measurements.

RECIPE 1: CRISPY AIR-FRIED FOODS

Cooking Time: 15 minutes Servings: 2

Ingredients:

- 250g (8.8 oz) boneless chicken tenders
- 1 cup (120g) breadcrumbs
- 1 teaspoon paprika
- 1 teaspoon garlic powder
- 1/2 teaspoon salt
- 1/4 teaspoon black pepper
- 1 egg, beaten
- Cooking spray

Instructions:
1. In a bowl, mix the breadcrumbs, paprika, garlic powder, salt, and black pepper.
2. Dip each chicken tender into the beaten egg, allowing excess to drip off, and then coat it with the breadcrumb mixture.
3. Preheat your air fryer to 200°C (392°F) for 5 minutes.
4. Place the coated chicken tenders in the air fryer basket in a single layer.
5. Lightly spray the chicken tenders with cooking spray.
6. Air fry for 10-12 minutes, flipping them halfway through, until they are golden brown and have an internal temperature of 75°C (165°F).
7. Serve your crispy air-fried chicken tenders with your favourite dipping sauce.

Nutrition Information (per serving):
- Calories: 320
- Protein: 22g
- Carbohydrates: 21g
- Fat: 16g
- Fiber: 1g

RECIPE 2: PERFECTLY ROASTED VEGETABLES

Cooking Time: 20 minutes Servings: 4

Ingredients:
- 500g (17.6 oz) mixed vegetables (e.g., carrots, bell peppers, zucchini, and cherry tomatoes)
- 2 tablespoons olive oil
- 1 teaspoon dried thyme
- 1/2 teaspoon salt
- 1/4 teaspoon black pepper

Instructions:
1. Preheat your air fryer to 180°C (356°F) for 5 minutes.
2. In a large bowl, toss the mixed vegetables with olive oil, dried thyme, salt, and black pepper until well coated.

3. Place the seasoned vegetables in the air fryer basket.
4. Air fry for 15-18 minutes, shaking the basket every 5 minutes, until the vegetables are tender and have crispy edges.
5. Serve your perfectly roasted vegetables as a side dish or a healthy snack.

Nutrition Information (per serving):
- Calories: 90
- Protein: 2g
- Carbohydrates: 10g
- Fat: 5g
- Fiber: 3g

RECIPE 3: GOLDEN BROWN FRIES AND CHIPS

Cooking Time: 20 minutes Servings: 2

Ingredients:
- 2 large potatoes, cut into fries or chips
- 1 tablespoon vegetable oil
- 1/2 teaspoon paprika
- 1/2 teaspoon garlic powder
- 1/2 teaspoon salt
- 1/4 teaspoon black pepper

Instructions:
1. Preheat your air fryer to 200°C (392°F) for 5 minutes.
2. In a large bowl, toss the potato fries or chips with vegetable oil, paprika, garlic powder, salt, and black pepper until well coated.
3. Place the seasoned potatoes in the air fryer basket in a single layer.
4. Air fry for 15-18 minutes, shaking the basket halfway through, until the fries or chips are golden brown and crispy.
5. Serve your golden-brown fries and chips with your favourite dipping sauce.

Nutrition Information (per serving):
- Calories: 220
- Protein: 3g
- Carbohydrates: 44g
- Fat: 5g
- Fiber: 5g

RECIPE 4: CLASSIC FISH AND CHIPS

Cooking Time: 20 minutes Servings: 4

Ingredients:
- 4 cod or haddock fillets
- 4 large potatoes, cut into chips
- 2 tablespoons vegetable oil
- Salt and pepper to taste
- Lemon wedges and tartar sauce for serving

Instructions:
1. Preheat your air fryer to 200°C (392°F) for 5 minutes.
2. Toss the potato chips with vegetable oil, salt, and pepper.
3. Place the chips and fish fillets in the air fryer basket, ensuring they are not overcrowded.
4. Air fry for 15-18 minutes, flipping the fish and shaking the basket halfway through, until the fish is golden brown and the chips are crispy.
5. Serve with lemon wedges and tartar sauce.

Nutrition Information (per serving):

- Calories: 450
- Protein: 30g
- Carbohydrates: 40g

- Fat: 18g
- Fiber: 5g

RECIPE 5: AIR-FRIED CHICKEN WINGS

Cooking Time: 25 minutes Servings: 4

Ingredients:
- 1 kg (35.3 oz) chicken wings
- 2 tablespoons baking powder
- 1 teaspoon paprika
- 1 teaspoon garlic powder
- 1/2 teaspoon salt
- 1/4 teaspoon black pepper
- Your choice of sauce (e.g., buffalo, BBQ, honey mustard)

Instructions:
1. Preheat your air fryer to 200°C (392°F) for 5 minutes.
2. In a bowl, combine the baking powder, paprika, garlic powder, salt, and black pepper.
3. Toss the chicken wings in the spice mixture until well coated.
4. Place the chicken wings in the air fryer basket.
5. Air fry for 20-23 minutes, shaking the basket halfway through, until the wings are crispy and have an internal temperature of 75°C (165°F).
6. Toss the wings in your preferred sauce and serve.

Nutrition Information (per serving):
- Calories: 450
- Protein: 30g
- Carbohydrates: 6g

- Fat: 34g
- Fiber: 1g

RECIPE 6: VEGGIE-PACKED MEATBALLS

Cooking Time: 15 minutes Servings: 4

Ingredients:
- 400g (14.1 oz) ground beef or turkey
- 1/4 cup breadcrumbs
- 1/4 cup grated zucchini
- 1/4 cup grated carrot
- 1/4 cup grated onion

- 1 egg
- 1/2 teaspoon Italian seasoning
- Salt and pepper to taste
- Tomato sauce for serving

Instructions:
1. In a bowl, combine the ground meat, breadcrumbs, grated vegetables, egg, Italian seasoning, salt, and pepper.
2. Form the mixture into meatballs.
3. Preheat your air fryer to 180°C (356°F) for 5 minutes.
4. Place the meatballs in the air fryer basket in a single layer.
5. Air fry for 12-15 minutes, turning the meatballs halfway through, until they are cooked through.

6. Serve with warm tomato sauce.

Nutrition Information (per serving):
- Calories: 220
- Protein: 20g
- Carbohydrates: 8g
- Fat: 12g
- Fiber: 2g

RECIPE 7: TASTY PORK CHOPS

Cooking Time: 15 minutes Servings: 2

Ingredients:
- 2 pork chops
- 2 tablespoons olive oil
- 1 teaspoon paprika
- 1/2 teaspoon garlic powder
- 1/2 teaspoon dried thyme
- Salt and pepper to taste

Instructions:
- Preheat your air fryer to 190°C (374°F) for 5 minutes.
- Rub the pork chops with olive oil and season with paprika, garlic powder, dried thyme, salt, and pepper.
- Place the pork chops in the air fryer basket.
- Air fry for 12-15 minutes, turning the chops halfway through, until they are cooked to your desired level of doneness.
- Let them rest for a few minutes before serving.

Nutrition Information (per serving):
- Calories: 280
- Protein: 25g
- Carbohydrates: 2g
- Fat: 19g
- Fiber: 1g

RECIPE 8: GARLIC PARMESAN BRUSSELS SPROUTS

Cooking Time: 15 minutes Servings: 4

Ingredients:
- 500g (17.6 oz) Brussels sprouts, trimmed and halved
- 2 tablespoons olive oil
- 2 cloves garlic, minced
- 1/4 cup grated Parmesan cheese
- Salt and pepper to taste

Instructions:
1. Preheat your air fryer to 180°C (356°F) for 5 minutes.
2. Toss the Brussels sprouts with olive oil, minced garlic, salt, and pepper.
3. Place the seasoned Brussels sprouts in the air fryer basket.
4. Air fry for 12-15 minutes, shaking the basket halfway through, until they are tender and slightly crispy.
5. Sprinkle with grated Parmesan cheese before serving.

Nutrition Information (per serving):
- Calories: 90
- Protein: 4g
- Carbohydrates: 8g
- Fat: 6g
- Fiber: 3g

RECIPE 9: SWEET POTATO FRIES

Cooking Time: 18 minutes Servings: 4

Ingredients:
- 4 medium sweet potatoes, cut into fries
- 2 tablespoons olive oil
- 1 teaspoon paprika
- 1/2 teaspoon garlic powder
- 1/2 teaspoon salt
- 1/4 teaspoon black pepper

Instructions:
- Preheat your air fryer to 190°C (374°F) for 5 minutes.
- Toss the sweet potato fries with olive oil, paprika, garlic powder, salt, and black pepper.
- Place the seasoned sweet potato fries in the air fryer basket.
- Air fry for 15-18 minutes, shaking the basket halfway through, until the fries are golden and crispy.
- Serve with your preferred dipping sauce.

Nutrition Information (per serving):
- Calories: 150
- Protein: 2g
- Carbohydrates: 25g
- Fat: 6g
- Fiber: 4g

RECIPE 10: EASY ONION RINGS

Cooking Time: 12 minutes Servings: 4

Ingredients:
- 2 large onions, cut into rings
- 1 cup (120g) breadcrumbs
- 1/2 cup (60g) all-purpose flour
- 1 teaspoon paprika
- 1/2 teaspoon garlic powder
- 1/2 teaspoon salt
- 1/4 teaspoon black pepper
- 1 egg, beaten
- Cooking spray

Instructions:
1. In a bowl, mix the breadcrumbs, flour, paprika, garlic powder, salt, and black pepper.
2. Dip each onion ring into the beaten egg, allowing excess to drip off, and then coat it with the breadcrumb mixture.
3. Preheat your air fryer to 190°C (374°F) for 5 minutes.
4. Place the coated onion rings in the air fryer basket.
5. Lightly spray the onion rings with cooking spray.
6. Air fry for 10-12 minutes, flipping them halfway through, until they are golden brown and crispy.
7. Serve with your favourite dipping sauce.

Nutrition Information (per serving):
- Calories: 200
- Protein: 6g
- Carbohydrates: 35g
- Fat: 4g
- Fiber: 3g

RECIPE 11: GRILLED CORN ON THE COB

Cooking Time: 12 minutes Servings: 4

Ingredients:
- 4 ears of corn, husked
- 2 tablespoons butter, melted
- Salt and pepper to taste

Instructions:
1. Preheat your air fryer to 180°C (356°F) for 5 minutes.
2. Brush each ear of corn with melted butter and season with salt and pepper.
3. Place the corn in the air fryer basket.
4. Air fry for 10-12 minutes, turning the corn halfway through, until it's tender and slightly charred.
5. Serve with additional melted butter, if desired.

Nutrition Information (per serving):
- Calories: 120
- Protein: 3g
- Carbohydrates: 19g
- Fat: 5g
- Fiber: 2g

RECIPE 12: CRISPY TOFU BITES

Cooking Time: 15 minutes Servings: 4

Ingredients:
- 400g (14.1 oz) extra-firm tofu, cubed
- 2 tablespoons soy sauce
- 1 tablespoon cornstarch
- 1 teaspoon paprika
- 1/2 teaspoon garlic powder
- 1/2 teaspoon ginger powder
- 1/4 teaspoon salt
- Cooking spray

Instructions:
1. In a bowl, combine the cubed tofu, soy sauce, cornstarch, paprika, garlic powder, ginger powder, and salt. Toss until well coated.
2. Preheat your air fryer to 200°C (392°F) for 5 minutes.
3. Place the marinated tofu cubes in the air fryer basket.
4. Lightly spray the tofu with cooking spray.
5. Air fry for 12-15 minutes, shaking the basket halfway through, until the tofu is crispy and golden brown.
6. Serve with a dipping sauce of your choice.

Nutrition Information (per serving):
- Calories: 120
- Protein: 8g
- Carbohydrates: 5g
- Fat: 8g
- Fiber: 1g

RECIPE 13: STUFFED BELL PEPPERS

Cooking Time: 20 minutes Servings: 4

Ingredients:

- 4 large bell peppers
- 250g (8.8 oz) ground beef or turkey
- 1 cup cooked rice
- 1/2 cup tomato sauce
- 1/2 teaspoon Italian seasoning
- Salt and pepper to taste
- Grated Cheddar cheese for topping

Instructions:

1. Cut the tops off the bell peppers and remove the seeds.
2. In a bowl, mix the cooked rice, ground meat, tomato sauce, Italian seasoning, salt, and pepper.
3. Stuff each bell pepper with the mixture.
4. Preheat your air fryer to 180°C (356°F) for 5 minutes.
5. Place the stuffed bell peppers in the air fryer basket.
6. Air fry for 18-20 minutes, or until the peppers are tender and the filling is cooked.
7. Sprinkle with grated Cheddar cheese and air fry for an additional 2-3 minutes until the cheese is melted.

Nutrition Information (per serving):

- Calories: 350
- Protein: 20g
- Carbohydrates: 30g
- Fat: 16g
- Fiber: 4g

RECIPE 14: SPINACH AND MUSHROOM QUESADILLAS

Cooking Time: 10 minutes Servings: 4

Ingredients:

- 8 small tortillas
- 200g (7.1 oz) baby spinach
- 200g (7.1 oz) mushrooms, sliced
- 1 onion, chopped
- 1 teaspoon olive oil
- 1 teaspoon garlic powder
- Salt and pepper to taste
- 200g (7.1 oz) shredded Cheddar cheese
- Sour cream and salsa for serving

Instructions:

1. In a skillet, heat the olive oil over medium heat. Sauté the onions, mushrooms, and baby spinach until they are tender. Season with garlic powder, salt, and pepper.
2. Lay out four tortillas and top each with the sautéed mixture and shredded Cheddar cheese.
3. Place another tortilla on top to create a sandwich.
4. Preheat your air fryer to 180°C (356°F) for 5 minutes.
5. Place the quesadillas in the air fryer basket, ensuring they are not overcrowded.
6. Air fry for 6-8 minutes, flipping them halfway through, until they are crispy and the cheese is melted.
7. Serve with sour cream and salsa.

Nutrition Information (per serving):

- Calories: 300
- Protein: 12g
- Carbohydrates: 30g
- Fat: 15g
- Fiber: 4g

RECIPE 15: CAULIFLOWER STEAKS

Cooking Time: 15 minutes Servings: 4

Ingredients:
- 2 large cauliflower heads
- 2 tablespoons olive oil
- 1 teaspoon smoked paprika
- 1/2 teaspoon garlic powder
- 1/2 teaspoon cumin
- 1/2 teaspoon salt
- 1/4 teaspoon black pepper

Instructions:
1. Remove the leaves and trim the stem of each cauliflower head to create "steaks" about 1-inch thick.
2. In a small bowl, combine the olive oil, smoked paprika, garlic powder, cumin, salt, and black pepper.
3. Brush the cauliflower steaks with the spice mixture.
4. Preheat your air fryer to 200°C (392°F) for 5 minutes.
5. Place the cauliflower steaks in the air fryer basket.
6. Air fry for 12-15 minutes, turning them halfway through, until they are tender and slightly charred.
7. Serve as a vegetarian main course or a side dish.

Nutrition Information (per serving):
- Calories: 100
- Protein: 4g
- Carbohydrates: 10g
- Fat: 6g
- Fiber: 5g

RECIPE 16: SWEET AND SAVORY BUTTERNUT SQUASH

Cooking Time: 15 minutes Servings: 4

Ingredients:
- 500g (17.6 oz) butternut squash, peeled and cubed
- 2 tablespoons olive oil
- 1 tablespoon honey
- 1/2 teaspoon dried rosemary
- Salt and pepper to taste

Instructions:
1. Preheat your air fryer to 190°C (374°F) for 5 minutes.
2. Toss the butternut squash cubes with olive oil, honey, dried rosemary, salt, and pepper.
3. Place the seasoned butternut squash in the air fryer basket.
4. Air fry for 12-15 minutes, shaking the basket halfway through, until the squash is tender and caramelized.

Nutrition Information (per serving):
- Calories: 120
- Protein: 1g
- Carbohydrates: 20g
- Fat: 5g
- Fiber: 4g

RECIPE 17: GARLIC AND HERB ROASTED POTATOES

Cooking Time: 20 minutes Servings: 4

Ingredients:
- 500g (17.6 oz) baby potatoes, halved
- 2 tablespoons olive oil
- 2 cloves garlic, minced
- 1/2 teaspoon dried thyme
- 1/2 teaspoon dried rosemary
- Salt and pepper to taste

Instructions:
1. Preheat your air fryer to 200°C (392°F) for 5 minutes.
2. Toss the halved baby potatoes with olive oil, minced garlic, dried thyme, dried rosemary, salt, and pepper.
3. Place the seasoned potatoes in the air fryer basket.
4. Air fry for 18-20 minutes, shaking the basket halfway through, until the potatoes are crispy and golden.

Nutrition Information (per serving):
- Calories: 150
- Protein: 2g
- Carbohydrates: 20g
- Fat: 7g
- Fiber: 2g

RECIPE 18: LEMON AND HERB SALMON

Cooking Time: 12 minutes Servings: 2

Ingredients:
- 2 salmon fillets
- 2 tablespoons olive oil
- Zest and juice of 1 lemon
- 1 teaspoon dried dill
- 1/2 teaspoon dried parsley
- Salt and pepper to taste

Instructions:
1. Preheat your air fryer to 180°C (356°F) for 5 minutes.
2. In a bowl, mix the olive oil, lemon zest, lemon juice, dried dill, dried parsley, salt, and pepper.
3. Brush the salmon fillets with the lemon and herb mixture.
4. Place the salmon in the air fryer basket.
5. Air fry for 10-12 minutes, or until the salmon flakes easily with a fork.

Nutrition Information (per serving):
- Calories: 300
- Protein: 30g
- Carbohydrates: 2g
- Fat: 19g
- Fiber: 1g

RECIPE 19: CHEESY ZUCCHINI FRITTERS

Cooking Time: 15 minutes Servings: 4

Ingredients:
- 2 large zucchinis, grated and excess moisture squeezed out
- 1 cup (120g) grated Cheddar cheese
- 1/4 cup breadcrumbs
- 2 cloves garlic, minced
- 2 eggs
- 1/2 teaspoon dried oregano
- Salt and pepper to taste
- Cooking spray

Instructions:
1. In a bowl, combine the grated zucchini, grated Cheddar cheese, breadcrumbs, minced garlic, eggs, dried oregano, salt, and pepper.
2. Preheat your air fryer to 190°C (374°F) for 5 minutes.
3. Form the mixture into fritters and place them in the air fryer basket.
4. Lightly spray the fritters with cooking spray.

5. Air fry for 12-15 minutes, flipping them halfway through, until they are golden and crispy.

Nutrition Information (per serving):
- Calories: 220
- Protein: 10g
- Carbohydrates: 10g
- Fat: 15g
- Fiber: 2g

RECIPE 20: APPLE AND CINNAMON DESSERT WRAPS

Cooking Time: 10 minutes Servings: 4

Ingredients:
- 4 small flour tortillas
- 2 apples, thinly sliced
- 2 tablespoons butter, melted
- 2 teaspoons ground cinnamon
- 1/4 cup brown sugar
- Vanilla ice cream for serving

Instructions:
1. In a bowl, combine the melted butter, ground cinnamon, and brown sugar.
2. Lay out the flour tortillas and brush each with the cinnamon and sugar mixture.
3. Place apple slices in the centre of each tortilla.
4. Fold the sides of the tortilla over the apples to create a wrap.
5. Preheat your air fryer to 180°C (356°F) for 5 minutes.
6. Place the wraps in the air fryer basket.
7. Air fry for 8-10 minutes, until the wraps are crispy and the apples are tender.
8. Serve with a scoop of vanilla ice cream.

Nutrition Information (per serving):
- Calories: 220
- Protein: 2g
- Carbohydrates: 40g
- Fat: 6g
- Fiber: 4

CHAPTER 5: STARTERS AND SNACKS

In this chapter, we'll explore a selection of delightful starters and snacks suitable for your air fryer. Each recipe comes with cooking time, servings, ingredients, instructions, and nutritional information in UK measurements.

RECIPE 1: HOMEMADE POTATO WEDGES

Cooking Time: 25 minutes Servings: 4

Ingredients:
- 4 large russet potatoes, cut into wedges
- 2 tablespoons olive oil
- 1 teaspoon paprika
- 1/2 teaspoon garlic powder
- 1/2 teaspoon dried oregano
- 1/2 teaspoon salt
- 1/4 teaspoon black pepper

Instructions:
1. Preheat your air fryer to 200°C (392°F) for 5 minutes.
2. Toss the potato wedges with olive oil, paprika, garlic powder, dried oregano, salt, and black pepper.
3. Place the seasoned potato wedges in the air fryer basket.
4. Air fry for 20-22 minutes, shaking the basket halfway through, until the wedges are golden and crispy.
5. Serve with your choice of dipping sauce.

Nutrition Information (per serving):
- Calories: 200
- Protein: 4g
- Carbohydrates: 40g
- Fat: 3g
- Fiber: 5g

RECIPE 2: MOZZARELLA STICKS

Cooking Time: 10 minutes Servings: 4

Ingredients:
- 12 mozzarella sticks
- 1 cup (120g) breadcrumbs
- 1 teaspoon dried basil
- 1/2 teaspoon garlic powder
- 1/2 teaspoon salt
- 1/4 teaspoon black pepper
- 2 eggs, beaten
- Cooking spray

Instructions:
1. In a bowl, mix the breadcrumbs, dried basil, garlic powder, salt, and black pepper.
2. Dip each mozzarella stick into the beaten eggs and then coat it with the breadcrumb mixture.
3. Preheat your air fryer to 200°C (392°F) for 5 minutes.
4. Place the coated mozzarella sticks in the air fryer basket.
5. Lightly spray the sticks with cooking spray.
6. Air fry for 8-10 minutes, or until they are golden and the cheese is melted.
7. Serve with marinara sauce.

Nutrition Information (per serving):
- Calories: 250
- Protein: 10g
- Carbohydrates: 25g
- Fat: 12g
- Fiber: 2g

RECIPE 3: CHICKEN TENDERS

Cooking Time: 15 minutes Servings: 4

Ingredients:
- 500g (17.6 oz) chicken tenders
- 1 cup (120g) breadcrumbs
- 1 teaspoon paprika
- 1/2 teaspoon garlic powder
- 1/2 teaspoon dried thyme
- 1/2 teaspoon salt
- 1/4 teaspoon black pepper
- 2 eggs, beaten
- Cooking spray

Instructions:
1. In a bowl, combine the breadcrumbs, paprika, garlic powder, dried thyme, salt, and black pepper.
2. Dip each chicken tender into the beaten eggs and then coat it with the breadcrumb mixture.
3. Preheat your air fryer to 200°C (392°F) for 5 minutes.
4. Place the coated chicken tenders in the air fryer basket.
5. Lightly spray the tenders with cooking spray.
6. Air fry for 12-15 minutes, flipping them halfway through, until they are golden brown and have an internal temperature of 75°C (165°F).
7. Serve with your favourite dipping sauce.

Nutrition Information (per serving):
- Calories: 280
- Protein: 25g
- Carbohydrates: 20g
- Fat: 10g
- Fiber: 2g

RECIPE 4: VEGETABLE SPRING ROLLS

Cooking Time: 10 minutes Servings: 4

Ingredients:
- 8 vegetable spring rolls
- 1 tablespoon vegetable oil
- Sweet chili sauce for dipping

Instructions:
1. Preheat your air fryer to 180°C (356°F) for 5 minutes.
2. Brush the spring rolls with vegetable oil.
3. Place the spring rolls in the air fryer basket.
4. Air fry for 8-10 minutes, turning them halfway through, until they are crispy and heated through.
5. Serve with sweet chili sauce for dipping.

Nutrition Information (per serving):
- Calories: 180
- Protein: 4g
- Carbohydrates: 22g
- Fat: 8g

- Fiber: 2g

RECIPE 5: CRISPY HALLOUMI FRIES

Cooking Time: 12 minutes Servings: 4

Ingredients:
- 250g (8.8 oz) halloumi cheese, cut into strips
- 1/2 cup (60g) breadcrumbs
- 1/2 teaspoon dried oregano
- 1/4 teaspoon garlic powder
- 1/4 teaspoon black pepper
- 1 egg, beaten
- Cooking spray

Instructions:
1. In a bowl, combine the breadcrumbs, dried oregano, garlic powder, and black pepper.
2. Dip each halloumi strip into the beaten egg and then coat it with the breadcrumb mixture.
3. Preheat your air fryer to 200°C (392°F) for 5 minutes.
4. Place the coated halloumi strips in the air fryer basket.
5. Lightly spray the halloumi fries with cooking spray.
6. Air fry for 10-12 minutes, or until they are golden and crispy.
7. Serve with tzatziki or marinara sauce.

Nutrition Information (per serving):
- Calories: 250
- Protein: 10g
- Carbohydrates: 14g
- Fat: 16g
- Fiber: 1g

RECIPE 6: SPICY BUFFALO CAULIFLOWER BITES

Cooking Time: 15 minutes Servings: 4

Ingredients:
- 500g (17.6 oz) cauliflower florets
- 2 tablespoons olive oil
- 1/4 cup hot sauce
- 1 teaspoon garlic powder
- 1/2 teaspoon paprika
- 1/2 teaspoon salt
- 1/4 teaspoon black pepper
- Blue cheese or ranch dressing for dipping

Instructions:
1. In a bowl, mix the cauliflower florets with olive oil, hot sauce, garlic powder, paprika, salt, and black pepper.
2. Preheat your air fryer to 200°C (392°F) for 5 minutes.
3. Place the seasoned cauliflower florets in the air fryer basket.
4. Air fry for 12-15 minutes, shaking the basket halfway through, until the cauliflower is tender and slightly crispy.
5. Serve with blue cheese or ranch dressing for dipping.

Nutrition Information (per serving):
- Calories: 140
- Protein: 4g
- Carbohydrates: 10g
- Fat: 10g
- Fiber: 3g

RECIPE 7: GARLIC PARMESAN WINGS

Cooking Time: 18 minutes Servings: 4

Ingredients:
- 12 chicken wings
- 2 tablespoons butter, melted
- 2 cloves garlic, minced
- 1/4 cup grated Parmesan cheese
- Salt and pepper to taste

Instructions:
1. In a bowl, combine the melted butter, minced garlic, grated Parmesan cheese, salt, and pepper.
2. Preheat your air fryer to 200°C (392°F) for 5 minutes.
3. Brush each chicken wing with the garlic and Parmesan mixture.
4. Place the wings in the air fryer basket.
5. Air fry for 16-18 minutes, flipping the wings halfway through, until they are golden and cooked through.
6. Serve with extra Parmesan cheese for sprinkling.

Nutrition Information (per serving):
- Calories: 280
- Protein: 20g
- Carbohydrates: 1g
- Fat: 21g
- Fiber: 0g

RECIPE 8: SPINACH AND FETA STUFFED MUSHROOMS

Cooking Time: 10 minutes Servings: 4

Ingredients:
- 12 large mushrooms, stems removed and reserved
- 1/2 cup chopped spinach
- 1/4 cup crumbled feta cheese
- 2 cloves garlic, minced
- 1 tablespoon olive oil
- Salt and pepper to taste

Instructions:
1. In a skillet, heat the olive oil over medium heat. Sauté the reserved mushroom stems, spinach, and minced garlic until they are tender. Season with salt and pepper.
2. Stuff each mushroom cap with the sautéed mixture and feta cheese.
3. Preheat your air fryer to 180°C (356°F) for 5 minutes.
4. Place the stuffed mushrooms in the air fryer basket.
5. Air fry for 8-10 minutes, or until the mushrooms are tender and the cheese is melted.

Nutrition Information (per serving):
- Calories: 90
- Protein: 4g
- Carbohydrates: 5g
- Fat: 6g
- Fiber: 1g

RECIPE 9: CRISPY ONION BHAJIS

Cooking Time: 12 minutes Servings: 4

Ingredients:
- 2 large onions, thinly sliced
- 1 cup (120g) gram flour (chickpea flour)
- 1 teaspoon ground cumin
- 1 teaspoon ground coriander
- 1/2 teaspoon chili powder
- 1/2 teaspoon turmeric
- 1/2 teaspoon salt
- 1/4 teaspoon baking soda
- Water (for batter)
- Cooking spray

Instructions:
1. In a bowl, mix the gram flour, ground cumin, ground coriander, chili powder, turmeric, salt, and baking soda.
2. Gradually add water and stir until you have a thick, smooth batter.
3. Preheat your air fryer to 190°C (374°F) for 5 minutes.
4. Dip each onion slice into the batter, allowing excess to drip off, and place it in the air fryer basket.
5. Lightly spray the bhajis with cooking spray.
6. Air fry for 10-12 minutes, flipping them halfway through, until they are crispy and golden.

Nutrition Information (per serving):
- Calories: 160
- Protein: 5g
- Carbohydrates: 30g
- Fat: 2g
- Fiber: 5g

RECIPE 10: BAKED AVOCADO FRIES

Cooking Time: 15 minutes Servings: 4

Ingredients:
- 2 avocados, cut into wedges
- 1/2 cup (60g) breadcrumbs
- 1/2 teaspoon paprika
- 1/2 teaspoon garlic powder
- 1/2 teaspoon salt
- 1/4 teaspoon black pepper
- 1 egg, beaten
- Cooking spray

Instructions:
1. In a bowl, combine the breadcrumbs, paprika, garlic powder, salt, and black pepper.
2. Dip each avocado wedge into the beaten egg and then coat it with the breadcrumb mixture.
3. Preheat your air fryer to 190°C (374°F) for 5 minutes.
4. Place the coated avocado fries in the air fryer basket.
5. Lightly spray the fries with cooking spray.
6. Air fry for 12-15 minutes, flipping them halfway through, until they are golden and crispy.
7. Serve with a dip of your choice.

Nutrition Information (per serving):
- Calories: 180
- Protein: 5g
- Carbohydrates: 15g
- Fat: 12g
- Fiber: 6g

RECIPE 11: MINI SAUSAGE ROLLS

Cooking Time: 15 minutes Servings: 4

Ingredients:
- 8 mini sausage rolls
- 1 egg, beaten (for egg wash)
- Sesame seeds for sprinkling

Instructions:
1. Preheat your air fryer to 180°C (356°F) for 5 minutes.
2. Brush each sausage roll with beaten egg.
3. Place the sausage rolls in the air fryer basket.
4. Air fry for 12-15 minutes, or until they are golden and cooked through.
5. Sprinkle with sesame seeds and serve with tomato ketchup or brown sauce.

Nutrition Information (per serving):
- Calories: 250
- Protein: 7g
- Carbohydrates: 15g
- Fat: 18g
- Fiber: 2g

RECIPE 12: PANKO-CRUSTED ASPARAGUS SPEARS

Cooking Time: 10 minutes Servings: 4

Ingredients:
- 200g (7.1 oz) asparagus spears, trimmed
- 1/2 cup (60g) panko breadcrumbs
- 1/2 teaspoon lemon zest
- 1/4 teaspoon garlic powder
- 1/4 teaspoon salt
- 1/4 teaspoon black pepper
- 1 egg, beaten
- Cooking spray

Instructions:
1. In a bowl, combine the panko breadcrumbs, lemon zest, garlic powder, salt, and black pepper.
2. Dip each asparagus spear into the beaten egg and then coat it with the breadcrumb mixture.
3. Preheat your air fryer to 190°C (374°F) for 5 minutes.
4. Place the coated asparagus spears in the air fryer basket.
5. Lightly spray the spears with cooking spray.
6. Air fry for 8-10 minutes, or until they are crisp and the asparagus is tender.
7. Serve with a lemon wedge.

Nutrition Information (per serving):
- Calories: 80
- Protein: 4g
- Carbohydrates: 10g
- Fat: 3g
- Fiber: 2g

RECIPE 13: GARLIC AND HERB MUSHROOMS

Cooking Time: 10 minutes Servings: 4

Ingredients:
- 250g (8.8 oz) button mushrooms, cleaned and halved
- 2 tablespoons butter, melted

- 2 cloves garlic, minced
- 1 teaspoon dried parsley
- Salt and pepper to taste

Instructions:
1. In a bowl, mix the melted butter, minced garlic, dried parsley, salt, and pepper.
2. Preheat your air fryer to 180°C (356°F) for 5 minutes.
3. Toss the halved mushrooms in the garlic and herb mixture.
4. Place the mushrooms in the air fryer basket.
5. Air fry for 8-10 minutes, or until the mushrooms are tender and aromatic.
6. Serve as a side dish or as a topping for grilled meats.

Nutrition Information (per serving):
- Calories: 80
- Protein: 2g
- Carbohydrates: 3g
- Fat: 7g
- Fiber: 1g

RECIPE 14: SWEET POTATO CHIPS

Cooking Time: 15 minutes Servings: 4

Ingredients:
- 2 large sweet potatoes, cut into thin strips
- 2 tablespoons olive oil
- 1/2 teaspoon paprika
- 1/2 teaspoon garlic powder
- 1/2 teaspoon salt
- 1/4 teaspoon black pepper

Instructions:
1. Preheat your air fryer to 190°C (374°F) for 5 minutes.
2. Toss the sweet potato strips with olive oil, paprika, garlic powder, salt, and black pepper.
3. Place the seasoned sweet potatoes in the air fryer basket.
4. Air fry for 12-15 minutes, shaking the basket halfway through, until the chips are crispy and golden.
5. Serve with a sprinkle of sea salt.

Nutrition Information (per serving):
- Calories: 120
- Protein: 2g
- Carbohydrates: 20g
- Fat: 4g
- Fiber: 4g

RECIPE 15: STUFFED BELL PEPPERS

Cooking Time: 20 minutes Servings: 4

Ingredients:
- 4 large bell peppers
- 250g (8.8 oz) ground beef or turkey
- 1 cup cooked rice
- 1/2 cup tomato sauce
- 1/2 teaspoon Italian seasoning
- Salt and pepper to taste
- Grated Cheddar cheese for topping

Instructions:
1. Cut the tops off the bell peppers and remove the seeds.
2. In a bowl, mix the cooked rice, ground meat, tomato sauce, Italian seasoning, salt, and pepper.

3. Stuff each bell pepper with the mixture.
4. Preheat your air fryer to 180°C (356°F) for 5 minutes.
5. Place the stuffed bell peppers in the air fryer basket.
6. Air fry for 18-20 minutes, or until the peppers are tender and the filling is cooked.
7. Sprinkle with grated Cheddar cheese and air fry for an additional 2-3 minutes until the cheese is melted.

Nutrition Information (per serving):
- Calories: 350
- Protein: 20g
- Carbohydrates: 30g
- Fat: 16g
- Fiber: 4g

RECIPE 16: BAKED BRIE WITH CRANBERRY SAUCE

Cooking Time: 10 minutes Servings: 4

Ingredients:
- 1 wheel of Brie cheese
- 1/2 cup cranberry sauce
- 2 tablespoons honey
- A handful of fresh cranberries
- Fresh rosemary sprigs
- Baguette slices for serving

Instructions:
1. Preheat your air fryer to 180°C (356°F) for 5 minutes.
2. Place the wheel of Brie in a heatproof dish.
3. Top the Brie with cranberry sauce and drizzle honey over it.
4. Add fresh cranberries and a few rosemary sprigs for flavour.
5. Place the dish in the air fryer basket.
6. Air fry for 8-10 minutes until the Brie is soft and gooey.
7. Serve with baguette slices for dipping.

Nutrition Information (per serving, not including baguette):
- Calories: 220
- Protein: 7g
- Carbohydrates: 20g
- Fat: 12g
- Fiber: 1g

RECIPE 17: ZESTY LEMON HERB SHRIMP

Cooking Time: 8 minutes Servings: 4

Ingredients:
- 500g (17.6 oz) large shrimp, peeled and deveined
- Zest and juice of 1 lemon
- 2 cloves garlic, minced
- 2 tablespoons olive oil
- 1 teaspoon dried parsley
- 1/2 teaspoon dried thyme
- Salt and pepper to taste

Instructions:
1. In a bowl, mix the lemon zest, lemon juice, minced garlic, olive oil, dried parsley, dried thyme, salt, and pepper.
2. Preheat your air fryer to 200°C (392°F) for 5 minutes.
3. Toss the shrimp in the lemon herb mixture.
4. Place the shrimp in the air fryer basket.

5. Air fry for 6-8 minutes until the shrimp are pink and cooked through.
6. Serve with rice or a green salad.

Nutrition Information (per serving):
- Calories: 170
- Protein: 25g
- Carbohydrates: 2g
- Fat: 7g
- Fiber: 0g

RECIPE 18: MINI BEEF WELLINGTONS

Cooking Time: 18 minutes Servings: 4

Ingredients:
- 4 beef fillet steaks (approximately 150g each)
- 1 sheet of puff pastry, thawed
- 1 egg, beaten (for egg wash)
- Salt and pepper to taste
- Cooking spray

Instructions:
1. Season the beef fillet steaks with salt and pepper.
2. Wrap each steak in a small square of puff pastry, sealing the edges with egg wash.
3. Preheat your air fryer to 200°C (392°F) for 5 minutes.
4. Place the mini Beef Wellingtons in the air fryer basket.
5. Lightly spray the Wellingtons with cooking spray.
6. Air fry for 16-18 minutes, or until the pastry is golden and the beef is cooked to your desired level.
7. Serve with a red wine sauce.

Nutrition Information (per serving):
- Calories: 380
- Protein: 30g
- Carbohydrates: 12g
- Fat: 23g
- Fiber: 1g

RECIPE 19: STICKY TOFFEE PUDDING

Cooking Time: 12 minutes Servings: 4

Ingredients:
- 200g (7.1 oz) pitted dates, chopped
- 1 cup (240ml) boiling water
- 1 teaspoon bicarbonate of soda
- 100g (3.5 oz) unsalted butter
- 200g (7.1 oz) brown sugar
- 2 large eggs
- 200g (7.1 oz) self-rising flour
- 1 teaspoon vanilla extract
- 1/2 teaspoon ground ginger
- 1/2 teaspoon ground cinnamon
- For the toffee sauce: 200g (7.1 oz) brown sugar, 150ml double cream, 50g (1.8 oz) unsalted butter

Instructions:
1. In a bowl, pour boiling water over the chopped dates and add the bicarbonate of soda. Set aside to cool.
2. In another bowl, beat together the butter and brown sugar until light and fluffy.

3. Gradually add the eggs, then fold in the flour, vanilla extract, ground ginger, and ground cinnamon.
4. Fold the date mixture into the batter.
5. Preheat your air fryer to 180°C (356°F) for 5 minutes.
6. Pour the batter into greased ramekins.
7. Air fry for 10-12 minutes until the pudding is set and a skewer comes out clean.
8. While the pudding is cooking, make the toffee sauce by heating the brown sugar, double cream, and butter in a saucepan over low heat until smooth.
9. Serve the sticky toffee pudding with the toffee sauce poured over the top.

Nutrition Information (per serving):
- Calories: 550
- Protein: 4g
- Carbohydrates: 80g
- Fat: 25g
- Fiber: 4g

RECIPE 20: CHOCOLATE LAVA CAKES

Cooking Time: 10 minutes Servings: 4

Ingredients:
- 100g (3.5 oz) dark chocolate
- 100g (3.5 oz) unsalted butter
- 2 eggs
- 2 egg yolks
- 50g (1.8 oz) caster sugar
- 30g (1 oz) plain flour
- 1/2 teaspoon vanilla extract
- A pinch of salt
- Icing sugar for dusting

Instructions:
1. Preheat your air fryer to 180°C (356°F) for 5 minutes.
2. In a microwave-safe bowl, melt the dark chocolate and unsalted butter together. Allow to cool slightly.
3. In a separate bowl, whisk the eggs, egg yolks, caster sugar, plain flour, vanilla extract, and a pinch of salt until well combined.
4. Gradually fold the melted chocolate mixture into the egg mixture until you have a smooth batter.
5. Divide the batter among four greased ramekins.
6. Place the ramekins in the air fryer basket.
7. Air fry for 8-10 minutes until the edges are set but the centres are still soft.
8. Carefully remove the ramekins from the air fryer and allow them to cool slightly.
9. Dust with icing sugar and serve with a scoop of vanilla ice cream.

Nutrition Information (per serving):
- Calories: 450
- Protein: 7g
- Carbohydrates: 30g
- Fat: 35g
- Fiber: 2g

CHAPTER 6: MAIN COURSES

In this chapter, we'll explore satisfying main course dishes for your air fryer. Each recipe includes cooking time, servings, ingredients, instructions, and nutritional information in UK measurements.

RECIPE 1: CLASSIC FISH AND CHIPS

Cooking Time: 15 minutes Servings: 4

Ingredients:
- For the Fish:
- 4 white fish fillets (such as cod or haddock)
- 150g (5.3 oz) plain flour
- 2 large eggs, beaten
- 150g (5.3 oz) breadcrumbs
- Salt and pepper to taste

For the Chips:
- 4 large potatoes, cut into chips
- 2 tablespoons vegetable oil
- Salt and vinegar (for serving)

Instructions:
1. Preheat your air fryer to 200°C (392°F) for 5 minutes.
2. Season the fish fillets with salt and pepper.
3. Dip each fillet into the plain flour, then into the beaten eggs, and finally into the breadcrumbs.
4. Place the breaded fish fillets in the air fryer basket.
5. Toss the potato chips with vegetable oil and place them in the air fryer basket as well.
6. Air fry for 12-15 minutes, turning the chips halfway through, until the fish is golden and the chips are crispy.
7. Serve with salt, vinegar, and your choice of sauce.

Nutrition Information (per serving):
- Calories: 450
- Protein: 25g
- Carbohydrates: 50g
- Fat: 15g
- Fiber: 5g

RECIPE 2: AIR-FRIED CHICKEN WINGS

Cooking Time: 20 minutes Servings: 4

Ingredients:
- 1 kg (2.2 lbs) chicken wings
- 1 tablespoon baking powder
- 1/2 teaspoon salt
- 1/2 teaspoon black pepper
- 1/2 teaspoon paprika
- 1/2 teaspoon garlic powder
- 1/2 teaspoon onion powder
- 1/2 teaspoon dried thyme
- 1/2 teaspoon dried oregano
- 1/2 teaspoon dried rosemary
- Your favourite hot sauce or barbecue sauce (for tossing)

Instructions:
1. Preheat your air fryer to 200°C (392°F) for 5 minutes.

2. In a large bowl, toss the chicken wings with baking powder, salt, black pepper, paprika, garlic powder, onion powder, dried thyme, dried oregano, and dried rosemary.
3. Place the seasoned chicken wings in the air fryer basket, making sure they don't overlap.
4. Air fry for 18-20 minutes, flipping them halfway through, until they are crispy and cooked through.
5. Toss the cooked wings in your favourite hot sauce or barbecue sauce before serving.

Nutrition Information (per serving):
- Calories: 350
- Protein: 30g
- Carbohydrates: 5g
- Fat: 22g
- Fiber: 1g

RECIPE 3: VEGGIE-PACKED MEATBALLS

Cooking Time: 15 minutes Servings: 4

Ingredients:
- 500g (17.6 oz) lean ground beef or turkey
- 1 small onion, finely chopped
- 1 small carrot, grated
- 1 small zucchini, grated
- 1 garlic clove, minced
- 1/2 cup (60g) breadcrumbs
- 1/4 cup grated Parmesan cheese
- 1/4 cup fresh parsley, chopped
- 1 egg
- Salt and pepper to taste

Instructions:
1. Preheat your air fryer to 180°C (356°F) for 5 minutes.
2. In a large bowl, combine the ground meat, chopped onion, grated carrot, grated zucchini, minced garlic, breadcrumbs, Parmesan cheese, chopped parsley, and the egg.
3. Season with salt and pepper and mix until well combined.
4. Shape the mixture into meatballs and place them in the air fryer basket.
5. Air fry for 12-15 minutes, shaking the basket halfway through, until the meatballs are browned and cooked through.
6. Serve with your choice of sauce and pasta or rice.

Nutrition Information (per serving, without pasta or rice):
- Calories: 250
- Protein: 20g
- Carbohydrates: 10g
- Fat: 14g
- Fiber: 2g

RECIPE 4: TASTY PORK CHOPS

Cooking Time: 18 minutes Servings: 4

Ingredients:
- 4 bone-in pork chops
- 2 tablespoons olive oil
- 1 teaspoon dried thyme
- 1 teaspoon dried rosemary
- 1 teaspoon garlic powder
- 1 teaspoon onion powder
- 1/2 teaspoon paprika
- Salt and black pepper to taste

Instructions:
1. Preheat your air fryer to 200°C (392°F) for 5 minutes.

2. Brush the pork chops with olive oil.
3. In a small bowl, mix together the dried thyme, dried rosemary, garlic powder, onion powder, paprika, salt, and black pepper.
4. Season the pork chops with the spice mixture, pressing it into the meat.
5. Place the seasoned pork chops in the air fryer basket.
6. Air fry for 16-18 minutes, turning them halfway through, until they are cooked to your desired level and have a golden crust.
7. Serve with your favourite side dishes.

Nutrition Information (per serving, without side dishes):
- Calories: 300
- Protein: 25g
- Carbohydrates: 1g
- Fat: 22g And Fiber: 0g

RECIPE 5: BEEF AND MUSHROOM PIE

Cooking Time: 25 minutes Servings: 4

Ingredients:
- 500g (1.1 lbs) lean beef, diced
- 200g (7 oz) mushrooms, sliced
- 1 onion, finely chopped
- 2 cloves garlic, minced
- 2 tablespoons olive oil
- 1 cup beef stock
- 2 tablespoons Worcestershire sauce
- 2 tablespoons plain flour
- 1 sheet puff pastry
- Salt and pepper to taste
- 1 egg, beaten (for egg wash)

Instructions:
1. Preheat your air fryer to 200°C (392°F) for 5 minutes.
2. In a large skillet, heat the olive oil over medium heat. Sauté the diced beef until browned, then remove it from the pan.
3. In the same skillet, sauté the chopped onion and minced garlic until translucent. Add the sliced mushrooms and cook until they release their moisture.
4. Stir in the plain flour, then gradually add the beef stock and Worcestershire sauce. Cook until the mixture thickens.
5. Return the cooked beef to the skillet and season with salt and pepper.
6. Pour the filling into a pie dish and cover with a sheet of puff pastry. Brush the pastry with beaten egg.
7. Place the pie in the air fryer basket.
8. Air fry for 20-25 minutes, or until the pastry is golden and the filling is bubbling.

Nutrition Information (per serving):
- Calories: 450
- Protein: 30g
- Carbohydrates: 25g
- Fat: 25g
- Fiber: 2g

RECIPE 6: HONEY GLAZED SALMON

Cooking Time: 10 minutes Servings: 4

Ingredients:
- 4 salmon fillets
- 3 tablespoons honey

- 2 tablespoons soy sauce
- 1 tablespoon olive oil
- 2 cloves garlic, minced
- 1 teaspoon ginger, grated
- Lemon wedges for serving

Instructions:
1. Preheat your air fryer to 180°C (356°F) for 5 minutes.
2. In a bowl, whisk together the honey, soy sauce, olive oil, minced garlic, and grated ginger.
3. Brush the salmon fillets with the honey glaze.
4. Place the salmon in the air fryer basket.
5. Air fry for 8-10 minutes until the salmon is cooked through and flakes easily.
6. Serve with lemon wedges.

Nutrition Information (per serving):
- Calories: 280
- Protein: 25g
- Carbohydrates: 10g
- Fat: 15g
- Fiber: 0g

RECIPE 7: RATATOUILLE

Cooking Time: 20 minutes Servings: 4

Ingredients:
- 1 small eggplant, diced
- 1 zucchini, diced
- 1 red bell pepper, diced
- 1 yellow bell pepper, diced
- 1 onion, diced
- 2 cloves garlic, minced
- 400g (14 oz) can have diced tomatoes
- 1 teaspoon dried thyme
- 1 teaspoon dried rosemary
- 2 tablespoons olive oil
- Salt and pepper to taste

Instructions:
1. Preheat your air fryer to 180°C (356°F) for 5 minutes.
2. In a large bowl, toss the diced eggplant, zucchini, red bell pepper, yellow bell pepper, onion, and minced garlic with olive oil.
3. Place the mixed vegetables in the air fryer basket.
4. Air fry for 18-20 minutes, stirring occasionally, until the vegetables are tender.
5. Stir in the diced tomatoes, dried thyme, dried rosemary, salt, and pepper. Air fry for an additional 2 minutes.
6. Serve as a side dish or over cooked pasta.

Nutrition Information (per serving, without pasta):
- Calories: 140
- Protein: 3g
- Carbohydrates: 18g
- Fat: 7g
- Fiber: 5g

RECIPE 8: VEGETABLE AND CHICKPEA CURRY

Cooking Time: 15 minutes Servings: 4

Ingredients:

- 400g (14 oz) can of chickpeas, drained and rinsed
- 1 onion, chopped
- 1 red bell pepper, chopped
- 1 yellow bell pepper, chopped
- 1 courgette (zucchini), chopped
- 2 cloves garlic, minced
- 400g (14 oz) can of diced tomatoes
- 200ml (7 fl oz) coconut milk
- 2 tablespoons curry paste
- 1 tablespoon olive oil
- Salt and pepper to taste
- Fresh coriander leaves for garnish
- Cooked rice or naan bread for serving

Instructions:
1. Preheat your air fryer to 180°C (356°F) for 5 minutes.
2. In a large bowl, toss the chopped onion, red bell pepper, yellow bell pepper, courgette, and minced garlic with olive oil.
3. Place the mixed vegetables in the air fryer basket.
4. Air fry for 12-15 minutes, stirring occasionally, until the vegetables are tender.
5. Stir in the chickpeas, diced tomatoes, coconut milk, and curry paste. Air fry for an additional 2-3 minutes.
6. Serve the vegetable and chickpea curry over cooked rice or with naan bread. Garnish with fresh coriander leaves.

Nutrition Information (per serving, without rice or naan):
- Calories: 330
- Protein: 9g
- Carbohydrates: 30g
- Fat: 20g and Fiber: 9g

RECIPE 9: BBQ PULLED PORK

Cooking Time: 25 minutes Servings: 4

Ingredients:
- 600g (1.3 lbs) pork shoulder, trimmed of excess fat
- 1 onion, chopped
- 2 cloves garlic, minced
- 200ml (7 fl oz) barbecue sauce
- 2 tablespoons brown sugar
- 1 tablespoon smoked paprika
- Salt and pepper to taste
- Burger buns or rolls for serving

Instructions:
1. Preheat your air fryer to 180°C (356°F) for 5 minutes.
2. Season the pork shoulder with salt, pepper, and smoked paprika.
3. Place the seasoned pork shoulder in the air fryer basket and air fry for 20-25 minutes until the pork is tender and can be easily pulled apart with two forks.
4. While the pork is cooking, heat olive oil in a saucepan over medium heat. Sauté the chopped onion and minced garlic until translucent.
5. Stir in the barbecue sauce and brown sugar. Simmer for a few minutes to thicken the sauce.
6. Once the pork is cooked, shred it with two forks and mix it with the barbecue sauce.
7. Serve the BBQ pulled pork on burger buns or rolls.

Nutrition Information (per serving, without buns):
- Calories: 320
- Protein: 25g
- Carbohydrates: 20g
- Fat: 15g
- Fiber: 2g

RECIPE 10: VEGETABLE STIR-FRY

Cooking Time: 12 minutes Servings: 4

Ingredients:
- 200g (7.1 oz) broccoli florets
- 1 red bell pepper, sliced
- 1 yellow bell pepper, sliced
- 1 courgette (zucchini), sliced
- 1 carrot, sliced
- 200g (7.1 oz) snow peas
- 2 tablespoons soy sauce
- 1 tablespoon oyster sauce
- 1 tablespoon vegetable oil
- 2 cloves garlic, minced
- 1 teaspoon ginger, grated
- Cooked rice or noodles for serving

Instructions:
1. Preheat your air fryer to 180°C (356°F) for 5 minutes.
2. In a large bowl, toss the broccoli florets, red bell pepper, yellow bell pepper, courgette, carrot, and snow peas with vegetable oil.
3. Place the mixed vegetables in the air fryer basket.
4. Air fry for 10-12 minutes, stirring occasionally, until the vegetables are tender.
5. In a small bowl, mix together the soy sauce, oyster sauce, minced garlic, and grated ginger.
6. Pour the sauce over the cooked vegetables and stir to coat.
7. Serve the vegetable stir-fry over cooked rice or noodles.

Nutrition Information (per serving, without rice or noodles):
- Calories: 90
- Protein: 4g
- Carbohydrates: 14g
- Fat: 3g
- Fiber: 5g

RECIPE 11: MUSHROOM STUFFED CHICKEN BREAST

Cooking Time: 18 minutes Servings: 4

Ingredients:
- 4 boneless, skinless chicken breasts
- 200g (7.1 oz) mushrooms, finely chopped
- 1 small onion, finely chopped
- 2 cloves garlic, minced
- 50g (1.8 oz) grated Cheddar cheese
- 1 tablespoon olive oil
- 1 teaspoon dried thyme
- 1 teaspoon dried rosemary
- Salt and pepper to taste

Instructions:
1. Preheat your air fryer to 180°C (356°F) for 5 minutes.
2. In a skillet, heat the olive oil over medium heat. Sauté the chopped onion and minced garlic until translucent. Add the chopped mushrooms and cook until they release their moisture.
3. Stir in the dried thyme, dried rosemary, salt, and pepper. Remove from heat and allow the mixture to cool.
4. Cut a pocket into each chicken breast and stuff them with the mushroom mixture and grated Cheddar cheese.
5. Place the stuffed chicken breasts in the air fryer basket.
6. Air fry for 16-18 minutes until the chicken is cooked through and the cheese is melted and bubbly.

Nutrition Information (per serving):
- Calories: 250
- Protein: 30g
- Carbohydrates: 5g
- Fat: 12g
- Fiber: 2g

RECIPE 12: CREAMY PESTO PASTA

Cooking Time: 10 minutes Servings: 4

Ingredients:
- 300g (10.6 oz) penne pasta
- 200ml (7 fl oz) double cream
- 3 tablespoons pesto sauce
- 50g (1.8 oz) grated Parmesan cheese
- Salt and pepper to taste
- Fresh basil leaves for garnish

Instructions:
1. Cook the penne pasta according to the package instructions until al dente. Drain and set aside.
2. In a saucepan, heat the double cream and pesto sauce over low heat, stirring until well combined.
3. Stir in the grated Parmesan cheese and season with salt and pepper.
4. Pour the creamy pesto sauce over the cooked pasta and toss to coat.
5. Preheat your air fryer to 180°C (356°F) for 5 minutes.
6. Place the pasta in an oven-safe dish and air fry for 8-10 minutes until the top is golden and bubbling.
7. Garnish with fresh basil leaves and serve.

Nutrition Information (per serving):
- Calories: 450
- Protein: 12g
- Carbohydrates: 40g
- Fat: 25g
- Fiber: 2g

RECIPE 13: VEGETARIAN SPRING ROLLS

Cooking Time: 10 minutes Servings: 4

Ingredients:
- 8 spring roll wrappers
- 200g (7.1 oz) bean sprouts
- 1 carrot, julienned
- 1 courgette (zucchini), julienned
- 100g (3.5 oz) rice vermicelli noodles, cooked
- 2 cloves garlic, minced
- 2 tablespoons soy sauce
- 1 tablespoon olive oil
- Sweet chili sauce for dipping

Instructions:
1. Preheat your air fryer to 180°C (356°F) for 5 minutes.
2. In a skillet, heat the olive oil over medium heat. Sauté the minced garlic until fragrant.
3. Add the bean sprouts, julienned carrot, and julienned courgette. Sauté until the vegetables are tender.
4. Stir in the cooked rice vermicelli noodles and soy sauce. Cook for an additional 2 minutes.

5. Place a spring roll wrapper on a clean surface, then add a portion of the vegetable and noodle mixture.
6. Fold the sides of the wrapper in, then roll up tightly.
7. Place the vegetarian spring rolls in the air fryer basket.
8. Air fry for 8-10 minutes until the spring rolls are crispy and golden.
9. Serve with sweet chili sauce for dipping.

Nutrition Information (per serving, without sauce):
- Calories: 180
- Protein: 4g
- Carbohydrates: 30g
- Fat: 4g
- Fiber: 3g

RECIPE 14: BEEF AND BROCCOLI STIR-FRY

Cooking Time: 15 minutes Servings: 4

Ingredients:
- 400g (14 oz) beef sirloin, thinly sliced
- 1 broccoli head, cut into florets
- 1 red bell pepper, sliced
- 2 cloves garlic, minced
- 2 tablespoons soy sauce
- 1 tablespoon oyster sauce
- 1 tablespoon olive oil
- 1 teaspoon ginger, grated
- Cooked rice for serving

Instructions:
1. Preheat your air fryer to 180°C (356°F) for 5 minutes.
2. In a large bowl, toss the thinly sliced beef with soy sauce and grated ginger. Allow it to marinate for a few minutes.
3. Place the marinated beef in the air fryer basket and air fry for 5-7 minutes until cooked to your preference. Remove and set aside.
4. In the same bowl, toss the broccoli florets and red bell pepper with olive oil.
5. Place the mixed vegetables in the air fryer basket and air fry for 7-10 minutes until tender.
6. While the vegetables are cooking, heat a skillet over medium heat and sauté the minced garlic.
7. Add the cooked beef to the skillet, along with oyster sauce. Cook for a few minutes to combine.
8. Serve the beef and broccoli stir-fry over cooked rice.

Nutrition Information (per serving, without rice):
- Calories: 280
- Protein: 25g
- Carbohydrates: 12g
- Fat: 15g
- Fiber: 5g

RECIPE 15: LEMON DRIZZLE CAKE

Cooking Time: 25 minutes Servings: 8

Ingredients:
- 200g (7.1 oz) self-raising flour
- 200g (7.1 oz) unsalted butter, softened
- 200g (7.1 oz) caster sugar
- 4 large eggs
- Zest and juice of 2 lemons
- 100g (3.5 oz) icing sugar

Instructions:
1. Preheat your air fryer to 180°C (356°F) for 5 minutes.

2. In a bowl, beat together the softened butter and caster sugar until light and fluffy.
3. Gradually add the eggs, one at a time, beating well after each addition.
4. Fold in the self-raising flour and the zest of 2 lemons.
5. Grease and line a cake tin with parchment paper. Pour the cake batter into the tin.
6. Place the cake tin in the air fryer basket.
7. Air fry for 20-25 minutes until the cake is golden and a skewer comes out clean.
8. While the cake is cooking, mix the lemon juice and icing sugar to make a drizzle.
9. Once the cake is cooked, drizzle the lemon icing over the top.

Nutrition Information (per serving):
- Calories: 400
- Protein: 5g
- Carbohydrates: 45g
- Fat: 20g
- Fiber: 1g

RECIPE 16: BAKED BRIE WITH CRANBERRY SAUCE

Cooking Time: 10 minutes Servings: 4

Ingredients:
- 1 wheel of Brie cheese
- 1/2 cup cranberry sauce
- 2 tablespoons honey
- A handful of fresh cranberries
- Fresh rosemary sprigs
- Baguette slices for serving

Instructions:
1. Preheat your air fryer to 180°C (356°F) for 5 minutes.
2. Place the wheel of Brie in a heatproof dish.
3. Top the Brie with cranberry sauce and drizzle honey over it.
4. Add fresh cranberries and a few rosemary sprigs for flavour.
5. Place the dish in the air fryer basket.
6. Air fry for 8-10 minutes until the Brie is soft and gooey.
7. Serve with baguette slices for dipping.

Nutrition Information (per serving, not including baguette):
- Calories: 220
- Protein: 7g
- Carbohydrates: 20g
- Fat: 12g
- Fiber: 1g

RECIPE 17: ZESTY LEMON HERB SHRIMP

Cooking Time: 8 minutes Servings: 4

Ingredients:
- 500g (17.6 oz) large shrimp, peeled and deveined
- Zest and juice of 1 lemon
- 2 cloves garlic, minced
- 2 tablespoons olive oil
- 1 teaspoon dried parsley
- 1/2 teaspoon dried thyme
- Salt and pepper to taste

Instructions:
1. In a bowl, mix the lemon zest, lemon juice, minced garlic, olive oil, dried parsley, dried thyme, salt, and pepper.
2. Preheat your air fryer to 200°C (392°F) for 5 minutes.

3. Toss the shrimp in the lemon herb mixture.
4. Place the shrimp in the air fryer basket.
5. Air fry for 6-8 minutes until the shrimp are pink and cooked through.
6. Serve with rice or a green salad.

Nutrition Information (per serving):
- Calories: 170
- Protein: 25g
- Carbohydrates: 2g
- Fat: 7g
- Fiber: 0g

RECIPE 18: MINI BEEF WELLINGTONS

Cooking Time: 18 minutes Servings: 4

Ingredients:
- 4 beef fillet steaks (approximately 150g each)
- 1 sheet of puff pastry, thawed
- 1 egg, beaten (for egg wash)
- Salt and pepper to taste
- Cooking spray

Instructions:
1. Season the beef fillet steaks with salt and pepper.
2. Wrap each steak in a small square of puff pastry, sealing the edges with egg wash.
3. Preheat your air fryer to 200°C (392°F) for 5 minutes.
4. Place the mini Beef Wellingtons in the air fryer basket.
5. Lightly spray the Wellingtons with cooking spray.
6. Air fry for 16-18 minutes, or until the pastry is golden and the beef is cooked to your desired level.
7. Serve with a red wine sauce.

Nutrition Information (per serving):
- Calories: 380
- Protein: 30g
- Carbohydrates: 12g
- Fat: 23g
- Fiber: 1g

RECIPE 19: STICKY TOFFEE PUDDING

Cooking Time: 12 minutes Servings: 4

Ingredients:
- 200g (7.1 oz) pitted dates, chopped
- 1 cup (240ml) boiling water
- 1 teaspoon bicarbonate of soda
- 100g (3.5 oz) unsalted butter
- 200g (7.1 oz) brown sugar
- 2 large eggs
- 200g (7.1 oz) self-raising flour
- 1 teaspoon vanilla extract
- 1/2 teaspoon ground ginger
- 1/2 teaspoon ground cinnamon
- For the toffee sauce: 200g (7.1 oz) brown sugar, 150ml double cream, 50g (1.8 oz) unsalted butter

Instructions:
1. In a bowl, pour boiling water over the chopped dates and add the bicarbonate of soda. Set aside to cool.

2. In another bowl, beat together the butter and brown sugar until light and fluffy.
3. Gradually add the eggs, then fold in the flour, vanilla extract, ground ginger, and ground cinnamon.
4. Fold the date mixture into the batter.
5. Preheat your air fryer to 180°C (356°F) for 5 minutes.
6. Grease a baking dish and pour the pudding batter into it.
7. Place the baking dish in the air fryer basket.
8. Air fry for 10-12 minutes until the pudding is springy and a skewer comes out clean.
9. While the pudding is cooking, make the toffee sauce by melting brown sugar, double cream, and unsalted butter in a saucepan over low heat.
10. Serve the sticky toffee pudding with warm toffee sauce.

Nutrition Information (per serving):
- Calories: 500
- Protein: 5g
- Carbohydrates: 65g
- Fat: 25g
- Fiber: 3g

CHAPTER 7: SIDES AND ACCOMPANIMENTS

In this chapter, we'll explore a selection of delectable sides and accompaniments to complement your main dishes. Each recipe includes cooking time, servings, ingredients, instructions, and nutritional information in UK measurements.

RECIPE 1: GARLIC PARMESAN BRUSSELS SPROUTS

Cooking Time: 15 minutes Servings: 4

Ingredients:
- 500g (17.6 oz) Brussels sprouts, trimmed and halved
- 2 tablespoons olive oil
- 2 cloves garlic, minced
- 50g (1.8 oz) grated Parmesan cheese
- Salt and black pepper to taste

Instructions:
1. Preheat your air fryer to 180°C (356°F) for 5 minutes.
2. In a bowl, toss the Brussels sprouts with olive oil and minced garlic.
3. Place the Brussels sprouts in the air fryer basket.
4. Air fry for 12-15 minutes, shaking the basket occasionally, until the sprouts are tender and golden.
5. Sprinkle with grated Parmesan cheese, salt, and black pepper. Air fry for an additional 1-2 minutes until the cheese is melted and bubbly.

Nutrition Information (per serving):
- Calories: 130
- Protein: 5g
- Carbohydrates: 10g
- Fat: 8g
- Fiber: 4g

RECIPE 2: SWEET POTATO FRIES

Cooking Time: 20 minutes Servings: 4

Ingredients:
- 4 medium sweet potatoes, cut into fries
- 2 tablespoons olive oil
- 1 teaspoon paprika
- 1/2 teaspoon garlic powder
- 1/2 teaspoon onion powder
- Salt and black pepper to taste

Instructions:
1. Preheat your air fryer to 180°C (356°F) for 5 minutes.
2. In a bowl, toss the sweet potato fries with olive oil, paprika, garlic powder, onion powder, salt, and black pepper.
3. Place the sweet potato fries in the air fryer basket.
4. Air fry for 18-20 minutes, shaking the basket occasionally, until the fries are crispy and cooked through.

Nutrition Information (per serving):
- Calories: 180
- Protein: 2g

- Carbohydrates: 30g
- Fat: 7g
- Fiber: 5g

RECIPE 3: EASY ONION RINGS

Cooking Time: 10 minutes Servings: 4

Ingredients:
- 2 large onions, sliced into rings
- 200g (7.1 oz) plain flour
- 2 large eggs, beaten
- 100g (3.5 oz) breadcrumbs
- 1 teaspoon paprika
- 1/2 teaspoon garlic powder
- Salt and black pepper to taste

Instructions:
1. Preheat your air fryer to 180°C (356°F) for 5 minutes.
2. In a bowl, mix the plain flour with paprika, garlic powder, salt, and black pepper.
3. Dip the onion rings into the flour mixture, then into the beaten eggs, and finally into the breadcrumbs, pressing them to adhere.
4. Place the coated onion rings in the air fryer basket.
5. Air fry for 8-10 minutes until the onion rings are golden and crispy.

Nutrition Information (per serving):
- Calories: 220
- Protein: 5g
- Carbohydrates: 35g
- Fat: 6g
- Fiber: 3g

RECIPE 4: GRILLED CORN ON THE COB

Cooking Time: 10 minutes Servings: 4

Ingredients:
- 4 corn cobs, husked
- 2 tablespoons butter, melted
- Salt and black pepper to taste
- Fresh parsley for garnish

Instructions:
1. Preheat your air fryer to 180°C (356°F) for 5 minutes.
2. Brush the corn cobs with melted butter and season with salt and black pepper.
3. Place the corn cobs in the air fryer basket.
4. Air fry for 8-10 minutes, turning them occasionally, until the corn is tender and lightly charred.
5. Garnish with fresh parsley before serving.

Nutrition Information (per serving):
- Calories: 120
- Protein: 2g
- Carbohydrates: 20g
- Fat: 5g
- Fiber: 3g

RECIPE 5: COURGETTE (ZUCCHINI) CHIPS

Cooking Time: 10 minutes Servings: 4

Ingredients:

- 2 courgettes (zucchinis), thinly sliced
- 2 tablespoons olive oil
- 50g (1.8 oz) grated Parmesan cheese
- 1 teaspoon dried oregano
- Salt and black pepper to taste

Instructions:
1. Preheat your air fryer to 180°C (356°F) for 5 minutes.
2. In a bowl, toss the thinly sliced courgette with olive oil, dried oregano, salt, and black pepper.
3. Place the courgette slices in the air fryer basket.
4. Air fry for 8-10 minutes until the courgette chips are crispy and golden.
5. Sprinkle with grated Parmesan cheese before serving.

Nutrition Information (per serving):
- Calories: 90
- Protein: 4g
- Carbohydrates: 5g
- Fat: 6g
- Fiber: 2g

RECIPE 6: ROASTED BUTTERNUT SQUASH

Cooking Time: 15 minutes Servings: 4

Ingredients:
- 1 butternut squash, peeled, seeded, and diced
- 2 tablespoons olive oil
- 1 teaspoon dried sage
- 1 teaspoon dried thyme
- Salt and black pepper to taste

Instructions:
1. Preheat your air fryer to 200°C (392°F) for 5 minutes.
2. In a bowl, toss the diced butternut squash with olive oil, dried sage, dried thyme, salt, and black pepper.
3. Place the butternut squash in the air fryer basket.
4. Air fry for 12-15 minutes until the squash is tender and slightly caramelized.

Nutrition Information (per serving):
- Calories: 90
- Protein: 1g
- Carbohydrates: 20g
- Fat: 2g
- Fiber: 4g

RECIPE 7: GARLIC MUSHROOMS

Cooking Time: 10 minutes Servings: 4

Ingredients:
- 300g (10.6 oz) button mushrooms, cleaned and halved
- 2 cloves garlic, minced
- 2 tablespoons butter
- 2 tablespoons fresh parsley, chopped
- Salt and black pepper to taste

Instructions:
1. Preheat your air fryer to 180°C (356°F) for 5 minutes.
2. In a bowl, toss the halved mushrooms with minced garlic, melted butter, salt, and black pepper.
3. Place the mushrooms in the air fryer basket.
4. Air fry for 8-10 minutes until the mushrooms are tender and golden.

5. Garnish with fresh parsley before serving.

Nutrition Information (per serving):
- Calories: 70
- Protein: 3g
- Carbohydrates: 3g
- Fat: 6g
- Fiber: 1g

RECIPE 8: CRISPY BATTERED FISH

Cooking Time: 12 minutes Servings: 4

Ingredients:
- 4 white fish fillets (e.g., cod or haddock)
- 150g (5.3 oz) plain flour
- 1 teaspoon baking powder
- 200ml (7 fl oz) sparkling water
- Salt and black pepper to taste

Instructions:
1. Preheat your air fryer to 200°C (392°F) for 5 minutes.
2. In a bowl, whisk together the plain flour, baking powder, sparkling water, salt, and black pepper until you have a smooth batter.
3. Dip each fish fillet into the batter, allowing any excess to drip off.
4. Place the battered fish fillets in the air fryer basket.
5. Air fry for 10-12 minutes until the fish is crispy and cooked through.

Nutrition Information (per serving):
- Calories: 220
- Protein: 25g
- Carbohydrates: 25g
- Fat: 2g
- Fiber: 1g

RECIPE 9: BREADED CHICKEN TENDERS

Cooking Time: 15 minutes Servings: 4

Ingredients:
- 500g (17.6 oz) chicken tenders
- 100g (3.5 oz) breadcrumbs
- 2 teaspoons paprika
- 1 teaspoon garlic powder
- 2 eggs, beaten
- Salt and black pepper to taste

Instructions:
1. Preheat your air fryer to 180°C (356°F) for 5 minutes.
2. In a bowl, combine the breadcrumbs with paprika, garlic powder, salt, and black pepper.
3. Dip each chicken tender into the beaten eggs and then into the breadcrumb mixture, pressing them to adhere.
4. Place the breaded chicken tenders in the air fryer basket.
5. Air fry for 12-15 minutes until the chicken tenders are golden and cooked through.

Nutrition Information (per serving):
- Calories: 250
- Protein: 20g
- Carbohydrates: 15g
- Fat: 12g
- Fiber: 2g

RECIPE 10: BEEF STIR-FRY

Cooking Time: 12 minutes Servings: 4

Ingredients:
- 400g (14 oz) beef strips
- 1 red bell pepper, sliced
- 1 green bell pepper, sliced
- 1 onion, sliced
- 2 cloves garlic, minced
- 2 tablespoons soy sauce
- 1 tablespoon olive oil
- 1 teaspoon ginger, grated
- Cooked rice or noodles for serving

Instructions:
1. Preheat your air fryer to 200°C (392°F) for 5 minutes.
2. In a large bowl, toss the beef strips with soy sauce and grated ginger.
3. Place the marinated beef in the air fryer basket and air fry for 5-7 minutes until cooked to your preference. Remove and set aside.
4. In the same bowl, toss the sliced red bell pepper, green bell pepper, onion, and minced garlic with olive oil.
5. Place the mixed vegetables in the air fryer basket and air fry for 5-7 minutes until tender.
6. While the vegetables are cooking, heat a skillet over medium heat and sauté the cooked beef strips along with any remaining marinade.
7. Combine the cooked beef with the air-fried vegetables.
8. Serve the beef stir-fry over cooked rice or noodles.

Nutrition Information (per serving, without rice or noodles):
- Calories: 280
- Protein: 25g
- Carbohydrates: 12g
- Fat: 15g
- Fiber: 5g

RECIPE 11: MUSHROOM STUFFED CHICKEN BREAST

Cooking Time: 18 minutes Servings: 4

Ingredients:
- 4 boneless, skinless chicken breasts
- 200g (7.1 oz) mushrooms, finely chopped
- 1 small onion, finely chopped
- 2 cloves garlic, minced
- 50g (1.8 oz) grated Cheddar cheese
- 1 tablespoon olive oil
- 1 teaspoon dried thyme
- 1 teaspoon dried rosemary
- Salt and black pepper to taste

Instructions:
1. Preheat your air fryer to 180°C (356°F) for 5 minutes.
2. In a skillet, heat the olive oil over medium heat. Sauté the chopped onion and minced garlic until translucent. Add the chopped mushrooms and cook until they release their moisture.
3. Stir in the dried thyme, dried rosemary, salt, and black pepper. Remove from heat and allow the mixture to cool.
4. Cut a pocket into each chicken breast and stuff them with the mushroom mixture and grated Cheddar cheese.
5. Place the stuffed chicken breasts in the air fryer basket.

6. Air fry for 16-18 minutes until the chicken is cooked through and the cheese is melted and bubbly.

Nutrition Information (per serving):
- Calories: 250
- Protein: 30g
- Carbohydrates: 5g
- Fat: 12g
- Fiber: 2g

RECIPE 12: CREAMY PESTO PASTA

Cooking Time: 10 minutes Servings: 4

Ingredients:
- 300g (10.6 oz) penne pasta
- 200ml (7 fl oz) double cream
- 3 tablespoons pesto sauce
- 50g (1.8 oz) grated Parmesan cheese
- Salt and black pepper to taste
- Fresh basil leaves for garnish

Instructions:
1. Cook the penne pasta according to the package instructions until al dente. Drain and set aside.
2. In a saucepan, heat the double cream and pesto sauce over low heat, stirring until well combined.
3. Stir in the grated Parmesan cheese and season with salt and black pepper.
4. Pour the creamy pesto sauce over the cooked pasta and toss to coat.
5. Preheat your air fryer to 180°C (356°F) for 5 minutes.
6. Place the pasta in an oven-safe dish and air fry for 8-10 minutes until the top is golden and bubbling.
7. Garnish with fresh basil leaves before serving.

Nutrition Information (per serving):
- Calories: 450
- Protein: 12g
- Carbohydrates: 40g
- Fat: 25g
- Fiber: 2g

RECIPE 13: VEGETARIAN SPRING ROLLS

Cooking Time: 10 minutes Servings: 4

Ingredients:
- 8 spring roll wrappers
- 200g (7.1 oz) bean sprouts
- 1 carrot, julienned
- 1 courgette (zucchini), julienned
- 100g (3.5 oz) rice vermicelli noodles, cooked
- 2 cloves garlic, minced
- 2 tablespoons soy sauce
- 1 tablespoon olive oil
- Sweet chili sauce for dipping

Instructions:
1. Preheat your air fryer to 180°C (356°F) for 5 minutes.
2. In a skillet, heat the olive oil over medium heat. Sauté the minced garlic until fragrant.
3. Add the bean sprouts, julienned carrot, and julienned courgette. Sauté until the vegetables are tender.
4. Stir in the cooked rice vermicelli noodles and soy sauce. Cook for an additional 2 minutes.

5. Place a spring roll wrapper on a clean surface, then add a portion of the vegetable and noodle mixture.
6. Fold the sides of the wrapper in, then roll up tightly.
7. Place the vegetarian spring rolls in the air fryer basket.
8. Air fry for 8-10 minutes until the spring rolls are crispy and golden.
9. Serve with sweet chili sauce for dipping.

Nutrition Information (per serving, without sauce):
- Calories: 180
- Protein: 4g
- Carbohydrates: 30g
- Fat: 4g
- Fiber: 3g

RECIPE 14: BEEF AND BROCCOLI STIR-FRY

Cooking Time: 15 minutes Servings: 4

Ingredients:
- 400g (14 oz) beef sirloin, thinly sliced
- 1 broccoli head, cut into florets
- 1 red bell pepper, sliced
- 2 cloves garlic, minced
- 2 tablespoons soy sauce
- 1 tablespoon oyster sauce
- 1 tablespoon olive oil
- 1 teaspoon ginger, grated
- Cooked rice for serving

Instructions:
1. Preheat your air fryer to 180°C (356°F) for 5 minutes.
2. In a large bowl, toss the thinly sliced beef with soy sauce and grated ginger. Allow it to marinate for a few minutes.
3. Place the marinated beef in the air fryer basket and air fry for 5-7 minutes until cooked to your preference. Remove and set aside.
4. In the same bowl, toss the broccoli florets and red bell pepper with olive oil.
5. Place the mixed vegetables in the air fryer basket and air fry for 7-10 minutes until tender.
6. While the vegetables are cooking, heat a skillet over medium heat and sauté the minced garlic.
7. Add the cooked beef to the skillet, along with oyster sauce. Cook for a few minutes to combine.
8. Serve the beef and broccoli stir-fry over cooked rice.

Nutrition Information (per serving, without rice):
- Calories: 280
- Protein: 25g
- Carbohydrates: 12g
- Fat: 15g
- Fiber: 5g

RECIPE 15: LEMON DRIZZLE CAKE

Cooking Time: 25 minutes Servings: 8

Ingredients:
- 200g (7.1 oz) self-raising flour
- 200g (7.1 oz) unsalted butter, softened
- 200g (7.1 oz) caster sugar
- 4 large eggs
- Zest and juice of 2 lemons
- 100g (3.5 oz) icing sugar

Instructions:
1. Preheat your air fryer to 180°C (356°F) for 5 minutes.

2. In a bowl, beat together the softened butter and caster sugar until light and fluffy.
3. Gradually add the eggs, one at a time, beating well after each addition.
4. Fold in the self-raising flour and the zest of 2 lemons.
5. Grease and line a cake tin with parchment paper. Pour the cake batter into the tin.
6. Place the cake tin in the air fryer basket.
7. Air fry for 20-25 minutes until the cake is golden and a skewer comes out clean.
8. While the cake is cooking, mix the lemon juice and icing sugar to make a drizzle.
9. Once the cake is cooked, drizzle the lemon icing over the top.

Nutrition Information (per serving):
- Calories: 400
- Protein: 5g
- Carbohydrates: 45g
- Fat: 20g
- Fiber: 1g

RECIPE 16: BAKED BRIE WITH CRANBERRY SAUCE
Cooking Time: 10 minutes Servings: 4

Ingredients:
- 1 wheel of Brie cheese
- 1/2 cup cranberry sauce
- 2 tablespoons honey
- A handful of fresh cranberries
- Fresh rosemary sprigs
- Baguette slices for serving

Instructions:
1. Preheat your air fryer to 180°C (356°F) for 5 minutes.
2. Place the wheel of Brie in a heatproof dish.
3. Top the Brie with cranberry sauce and drizzle honey over it.
4. Add fresh cranberries and a few rosemary sprigs for flavour.
5. Place the dish in the air fryer basket.
6. Air fry for 8-10 minutes until the Brie is soft and gooey.
7. Serve with baguette slices for dipping.

Nutrition Information (per serving, not including baguette):
- Calories: 220
- Protein: 7g
- Carbohydrates: 20g
- Fat: 12g
- Fiber: 1g

RECIPE 17: ZESTY LEMON HERB SHRIMP
Cooking Time: 8 minutes Servings: 4

Ingredients:
- 500g (17.6 oz) large shrimp, peeled and deveined
- Zest and juice of 1 lemon
- 2 cloves garlic, minced
- 2 tablespoons olive oil
- 1 teaspoon dried parsley
- 1/2 teaspoon dried thyme
- Salt and pepper to taste

Instructions:
1. In a bowl, mix the lemon zest, lemon juice, minced garlic, olive oil, dried parsley, dried thyme, salt, and pepper.

2. Preheat your air fryer to 200°C (392°F) for 5 minutes.
3. Toss the shrimp in the lemon herb mixture.
4. Place the shrimp in the air fryer basket.
5. Air fry for 6-8 minutes until the shrimp are pink and cooked through.
6. Serve with rice or a green salad.

Nutrition Information (per serving):
- Calories: 170
- Protein: 25g
- Carbohydrates: 2g
- Fat: 7g
- Fiber: 0g

RECIPE 18: MINI BEEF WELLINGTONS

Cooking Time: 18 minutes Servings: 4

Ingredients:
- 4 beef fillet steaks (approximately 150g each)
- 1 sheet of puff pastry, thawed
- 1 egg, beaten (for egg wash)
- Salt and pepper to taste
- Cooking spray

Instructions:
1. Season the beef fillet steaks with salt and pepper.
2. Wrap each steak in a small square of puff pastry, sealing the edges with egg wash.
3. Preheat your air fryer to 200°C (392°F) for 5 minutes.
4. Place the mini Beef Wellingtons in the air fryer basket.
5. Lightly spray the Wellingtons with cooking spray.
6. Air fry for 16-18 minutes, or until the pastry is golden and the beef is cooked to your desired level.
7. Serve with a red wine sauce.

Nutrition Information (per serving):
- Calories: 380
- Protein: 30g
- Carbohydrates: 12g
- Fat: 23g
- Fiber: 1g

RECIPE 19: STICKY TOFFEE PUDDING

Cooking Time: 12 minutes Servings: 4

Ingredients:
- 200g (7.1 oz) pitted dates, chopped
- 1 cup (240ml) boiling water
- 1 teaspoon bicarbonate of soda
- 100g (3.5 oz) unsalted butter
- 200g (7.1 oz) brown sugar
- 2 large eggs
- 200g (7.1 oz) self-rising flour
- 1 teaspoon vanilla extract
- 1/2 teaspoon ground ginger
- 1/2 teaspoon ground cinnamon
- For the toffee sauce: 200g (7.1 oz) brown sugar, 150ml double cream, 50g (1.8 oz) unsalted butter

Instructions:
1. In a bowl, pour boiling water over the chopped dates and add the bicarbonate of soda. Set aside to cool.

2. In another bowl, beat together the butter and brown sugar until light and fluffy.
3. Gradually add the eggs, then fold in the flour, vanilla extract, ground ginger, and ground cinnamon.
4. Fold the date mixture into the batter.
5. Preheat your air fryer to 180°C (356°F) for 5 minutes.
6. Grease a baking dish and pour the pudding batter into it.
7. Place the baking dish in the air fryer basket.
8. Air fry for 10-12 minutes until the pudding is springy and a skewer comes out clean.
9. While the pudding is cooking, make the toffee sauce by melting brown sugar, double cream, and unsalted butter in a saucepan over low heat.
10. Serve the sticky toffee pudding with warm toffee sauce.

Nutrition Information (per serving):
- Calories: 500
- Protein: 5g
- Carbohydrates: 65g
- Fat: 25g
- Fiber: 3g

RECIPE 20: FRUIT CRUMBLE

Cooking Time: 15 minutes Servings: 6

Ingredients:
- 500g (17.6 oz) mixed berries (e.g., strawberries, raspberries, blueberries)
- 200g (7.1 oz) granulated sugar
- 150g (5.3 oz) plain flour
- 100g (3.5 oz) unsalted butter
- 50g (1.8 oz) rolled oats
- 1 teaspoon ground cinnamon
- Custard or vanilla ice cream for serving

Instructions:
1. In a bowl, mix the mixed berries with 50g of granulated sugar.
2. Preheat your air fryer to 180°C (356°F) for 5 minutes.
3. In another bowl, combine the plain flour, unsalted butter, rolled oats, the remaining granulated sugar, and ground cinnamon. Rub the mixture together until it resembles breadcrumbs.
4. Place the mixed berries in an oven-safe dish and top with the crumble mixture.
5. Place the dish in the air fryer basket.
6. Air fry for 12-15 minutes until the crumble is golden and the fruit is bubbling.
7. Serve with custard or vanilla ice cream.

Nutrition Information (per serving, without custard or ice cream):
- Calories: 300
- Protein: 3g
- Carbohydrates: 45g
- Fat: 12g
- Fiber: 5g

CHAPTER 8: VEGETARIAN DELIGHTS

In this chapter, we're diving into a delectable array of vegetarian dishes, all prepared with the convenience of your air fryer. Each recipe includes cooking time, servings, ingredients, instructions, and nutritional information in UK measurements.

RECIPE 1: CRISPY TOFU BITES

Cooking Time: 15 minutes Servings: 4

Ingredients:
- 400g (14 oz) firm tofu, cut into bite-sized cubes
- 2 tablespoons soy sauce
- 2 tablespoons corn-starch
- 1/2 teaspoon garlic powder
- 1/2 teaspoon onion powder
- Cooking spray
- Sweet chili dipping sauce

Instructions:
1. Preheat your air fryer to 200°C (392°F) for 5 minutes.
2. In a bowl, toss the tofu cubes with soy sauce, corn-starch, garlic powder, and onion powder.
3. Lightly grease the air fryer basket with cooking spray.
4. Place the tofu cubes in the basket, ensuring they're not touching.
5. Air fry for 12-15 minutes, turning them occasionally, until the tofu is crispy and golden.
6. Serve with sweet chili dipping sauce.

Nutrition Information (per serving, without sauce):
- Calories: 130
- Protein: 9g
- Carbohydrates: 6g
- Fat: 8g
- Fiber: 2g

RECIPE 2: STUFFED BELL PEPPERS

Cooking Time: 20 minutes Servings: 4

Ingredients:
- 4 bell peppers, any color
- 200g (7.1 oz) cooked quinoa
- 200g (7.1 oz) black beans, drained and rinsed
- 200g (7.1 oz) sweetcorn kernels
- 1 small red onion, finely chopped
- 2 cloves garlic, minced
- 1 teaspoon cumin
- 1/2 teaspoon chili powder
- 200g (7.1 oz) grated Cheddar cheese
- Salt and black pepper to taste

Instructions:
1. Preheat your air fryer to 180°C (356°F) for 5 minutes.
2. Cut the tops off the bell peppers and remove the seeds and membranes.
3. In a large bowl, mix the cooked quinoa, black beans, sweetcorn, red onion, minced garlic, cumin, chili powder, half of the grated Cheddar cheese, salt, and black pepper.
4. Stuff the bell peppers with the quinoa mixture and top with the remaining cheese.
5. Place the stuffed bell peppers in the air fryer basket.

6. Air fry for 18-20 minutes until the peppers are tender and the cheese is melted and bubbly.

Nutrition Information (per serving):
- Calories: 320
- Protein: 15g
- Carbohydrates: 40g
- Fat: 12g
- Fiber: 9g

RECIPE 3: SPINACH AND MUSHROOM QUESADILLAS

Cooking Time: 10 minutes Servings: 4

Ingredients:
- 8 small flour tortillas
- 200g (7.1 oz) mushrooms, sliced
- 200g (7.1 oz) baby spinach
- 200g (7.1 oz) grated mozzarella cheese
- 1 tablespoon olive oil
- Salt and black pepper to taste
- Sour cream and salsa for serving

Instructions:
1. Preheat your air fryer to 180°C (356°F) for 5 minutes.
2. In a skillet, heat the olive oil over medium heat. Sauté the sliced mushrooms until they release their moisture and turn golden.
3. Add the baby spinach and sauté until wilted. Season with salt and black pepper.
4. Place one tortilla in the air fryer basket.
5. Spread a portion of the sautéed mushrooms and spinach over the tortilla and sprinkle with grated mozzarella cheese.
6. Top with another tortilla to make a quesadilla sandwich.
7. Air fry for 4-5 minutes until the quesadilla is crispy and the cheese is melted. Repeat for the remaining quesadillas.
8. Cut into wedges and serve with sour cream and salsa.

Nutrition Information (per serving, without sour cream and salsa):
- Calories: 250
- Protein: 10g
- Carbohydrates: 25g
- Fat: 12g
- Fiber: 2g

RECIPE 4: CAULIFLOWER STEAKS

Cooking Time: 15 minutes Servings: 4

Ingredients:
- 1 large cauliflower head
- 4 tablespoons olive oil
- 2 teaspoons paprika
- 1 teaspoon garlic powder
-
- 1 teaspoon dried thyme
- Salt and black pepper to taste
- Fresh parsley for garnish

Instructions:
1. Preheat your air fryer to 200°C (392°F) for 5 minutes.
2. Remove the leaves and stem from the cauliflower, leaving the core intact.
3. Cut the cauliflower into thick slices to create "steaks."

4. In a bowl, mix together the olive oil, paprika, garlic powder, dried thyme, salt, and black pepper.
5. Brush both sides of the cauliflower steaks with the seasoned oil.
6. Place the cauliflower steaks in the air fryer basket.
7. Air fry for 12-15 minutes, flipping them once, until they are tender and nicely charred.
8. Garnish with fresh parsley before serving.

Nutrition Information (per serving):
- Calories: 90
- Protein: 3g
- Carbohydrates: 7g
- Fat: 7g
- Fiber: 4g

RECIPE 5: CHEESY GARLIC BREAD

Cooking Time: 5 minutes Servings: 4

Ingredients:
- 4 slices of crusty bread
- 50g (1.8 oz) unsalted butter, softened
- 2 cloves of garlic, minced
- 100g (3.5 oz) grated Cheddar cheese
- Fresh parsley, chopped, for garnish

Instructions:
1. Preheat your air fryer to 180°C (356°F) for 5 minutes.
2. In a bowl, mix the softened butter with minced garlic.
3. Spread the garlic butter on the slices of bread and sprinkle with grated Cheddar cheese.
4. Place the prepared bread slices in the air fryer basket.
5. Air fry for 3-5 minutes until the bread is crispy and the cheese is bubbly.
6. Garnish with chopped fresh parsley before serving.

Nutrition Information (per serving):
- Calories: 250
- Protein: 10g
- Carbohydrates: 15g
- Fat: 16g
- Fiber: 2g

RECIPE 6: CLASSIC SHEPHERD'S PIE

Cooking Time: 15 minutes Servings: 4

Ingredients:
- 500g (17.6 oz) minced lamb or beef
- 1 onion, chopped
- 2 carrots, diced
- 2 cloves of garlic, minced
- 200g (7.1 oz) frozen peas
- 400g (14 oz) mashed potatoes
- 1 tablespoon Worcestershire sauce
- Salt and black pepper to taste
- Fresh thyme leaves for garnish

Instructions:
1. Preheat your air fryer to 200°C (392°F) for 5 minutes.
2. In a skillet, brown the minced lamb or beef over medium heat, breaking it into small pieces. Drain any excess fat.
3. Add the chopped onion, diced carrots, minced garlic, and frozen peas to the skillet. Cook until the vegetables are tender.

4. Stir in the Worcestershire sauce and season with salt and black pepper.
5. Transfer the meat and vegetable mixture to an oven-safe dish.
6. Spread the mashed potatoes on top.
7. Place the dish in the air fryer basket.
8. Air fry for 12-15 minutes until the top is golden and the filling is bubbling.
9. Garnish with fresh thyme leaves before serving.

Nutrition Information (per serving):
- Calories: 450
- Protein: 25g
- Carbohydrates: 25g
- Fat: 28g
- Fiber: 4g

RECIPE 7: SPICY CHICKEN DRUMSTICKS

Cooking Time: 20 minutes Servings: 4

Ingredients:
- 8 chicken drumsticks
- 2 tablespoons olive oil
- 1 teaspoon paprika
- 1/2 teaspoon cayenne pepper
- 1/2 teaspoon garlic powder
- Salt and black pepper to taste
- Fresh coriander leaves for garnish

Instructions:
1. Preheat your air fryer to 200°C (392°F) for 5 minutes.
2. In a bowl, toss the chicken drumsticks with olive oil, paprika, cayenne pepper, garlic powder, salt, and black pepper.
3. Place the seasoned drumsticks in the air fryer basket.
4. Air fry for 18-20 minutes until the chicken is crispy and fully cooked.
5. Garnish with fresh coriander leaves before serving.

Nutrition Information (per serving):
- Calories: 250
- Protein: 25g
- Carbohydrates: 2g
- Fat: 16g
- Fiber: 1g

RECIPE 8: HONEY GLAZED CARROTS

Cooking Time: 10 minutes Servings: 4

Ingredients:
- 500g (17.6 oz) baby carrots
- 2 tablespoons honey
- 2 tablespoons unsalted butter
- 1 teaspoon dried thyme
- Salt and black pepper to taste

Instructions:
1. Preheat your air fryer to 180°C (356°F) for 5 minutes.
2. In a bowl, mix the baby carrots with honey, unsalted butter, dried thyme, salt, and black pepper.
3. Place the seasoned carrots in the air fryer basket.
4. Air fry for 8-10 minutes until the carrots are tender and glazed.
5. Serve as a sweet and savoury side dish.

Nutrition Information (per serving):

- Calories: 120
- Protein: 1g
- Carbohydrates: 20g
- Fat: 6g
- Fiber: 4g

RECIPE 9: SALMON WITH LEMON-DILL SAUCE

Cooking Time: 12 minutes Servings: 4

Ingredients:

- 4 salmon fillets
- Zest and juice of 1 lemon
- 2 cloves garlic, minced
- 2 tablespoons olive oil
- 1 teaspoon dried dill
- Salt and black pepper to taste
- Fresh dill for garnish

Instructions:

1. Preheat your air fryer to 200°C (392°F) for 5 minutes.
2. In a bowl, mix the lemon zest, lemon juice, minced garlic, olive oil, dried dill, salt, and black pepper.
3. Brush the salmon fillets with the lemon-dill mixture.
4. Place the salmon in the air fryer basket.
5. Air fry for 10-12 minutes until the salmon is cooked through and flakes easily.
6. Garnish with fresh dill before serving.

Nutrition Information (per serving):

- Calories: 250
- Protein: 25g
- Carbohydrates: 1g
- Fat: 16g
- Fiber: 0g

RECIPE 10: VEGETABLE PAKORAS

Cooking Time: 8 minutes Servings: 4

Ingredients:

- 1 cup chickpea flour
- 1 teaspoon ground cumin
- 1 teaspoon ground coriander
- 1/2 teaspoon garam masala
- 1/2 teaspoon turmeric
- 1/2 teaspoon red chili powder
- 1 teaspoon salt
- 1/2 cup water
- 200g (7.1 oz) mixed vegetables (e.g., onions, bell peppers, cauliflower), thinly sliced
- Cooking oil spray

Instructions:

1. Preheat your air fryer to 180°C (356°F) for 5 minutes.
2. In a bowl, mix the chickpea flour, ground cumin, ground coriander, garam masala, turmeric, red chili powder, salt, and water to form a thick batter.
3. Dip the sliced vegetables into the batter to coat them evenly.
4. Place the coated vegetables in the air fryer basket.
5. Lightly spray them with cooking oil.
6. Air fry for 6-8 minutes until the pakoras are crispy and golden.
7. Serve with chutney or yogurt sauce.

Nutrition Information (per serving, without chutney or sauce):
- Calories: 150
- Protein: 4g
- Carbohydrates: 25g
- Fat: 3g
- Fiber: 5g

RECIPE 11: STUFFED CHICKEN BREASTS

Cooking Time: 18 minutes Servings: 4

Ingredients:
- 4 boneless, skinless chicken breasts
- 200g (7.1 oz) mushrooms, finely chopped
- 1 small onion, finely chopped
- 2 cloves garlic, minced
- 50g (1.8 oz) grated Cheddar cheese
- 1 tablespoon olive oil
- 1 teaspoon dried thyme
- 1 teaspoon dried rosemary
- Salt and black pepper to taste

Instructions:
1. Preheat your air fryer to 180°C (356°F) for 5 minutes.
2. In a skillet, heat the olive oil over medium heat. Sauté the chopped onion and minced garlic until translucent. Add the chopped mushrooms and cook until they release their moisture.
3. Stir in the dried thyme, dried rosemary, salt, and black pepper. Remove from heat and allow the mixture to cool.
4. Cut a pocket into each chicken breast and stuff them with the mushroom mixture and grated Cheddar cheese.
5. Place the stuffed chicken breasts in the air fryer basket.
6. Air fry for 16-18 minutes until the chicken is cooked through and the cheese is melted and bubbly.

Nutrition Information (per serving):
- Calories: 250
- Protein: 30g
- Carbohydrates: 5g
- Fat: 12g
- Fiber: 2g

RECIPE 12: CREAMY PESTO PASTA

Cooking Time: 10 minutes Servings: 4

Ingredients:
- 300g (10.6 oz) penne pasta
- 200ml (7 fl oz) double cream
- 3 tablespoons pesto sauce
- 50g (1.8 oz) grated Parmesan cheese
- Salt and black pepper to taste
- Fresh basil leaves for garnish

Instructions:
1. Cook the penne pasta according to the package instructions until al dente. Drain and set aside.
2. In a saucepan, heat the double cream and pesto sauce over low heat, stirring until well combined.
3. Stir in the grated Parmesan cheese and season with salt and black pepper.
4. Pour the creamy pesto sauce over the cooked pasta and toss to coat.
5. Preheat your air fryer to 180°C (356°F) for 5 minutes.

6. Place the pasta in an oven-safe dish and air fry for 8-10 minutes until the top is golden and bubbling.
7. Garnish with fresh basil leaves before serving.

Nutrition Information (per serving):
- Calories: 450
- Protein: 12g
- Carbohydrates: 40g
- Fat: 25g
- Fiber: 2g

RECIPE 13: VEGETARIAN SPRING ROLLS

Cooking Time: 10 minutes Servings: 4

Ingredients:
- 8 spring roll wrappers
- 200g (7.1 oz) bean sprouts
- 1 carrot, julienned
- 1 courgette (zucchini), julienned
- 100g (3.5 oz) rice vermicelli noodles, cooked
- 2 cloves garlic, minced
- 2 tablespoons soy sauce
- 1 tablespoon olive oil
- Sweet chili sauce for dipping

Instructions:
1. Preheat your air fryer to 180°C (356°F) for 5 minutes.
2. In a skillet, heat the olive oil over medium heat. Sauté the minced garlic until fragrant.
3. Add the bean sprouts, julienned carrot, and julienned courgette. Sauté until the vegetables are tender.
4. Stir in the cooked rice vermicelli noodles and soy sauce. Cook for an additional 2 minutes.
5. Place a spring roll wrapper on a clean surface, then add a portion of the vegetable and noodle mixture.
6. Fold the sides of the wrapper in, then roll up tightly.
7. Place the vegetarian spring rolls in the air fryer basket.
8. Air fry for 8-10 minutes until the spring rolls are crispy and golden.
9. Serve with sweet chili sauce for dipping.

Nutrition Information (per serving, without sauce):
- Calories: 180
- Protein: 4g
- Carbohydrates: 30g
- Fat: 4g
- Fiber: 3g

RECIPE 14: BEEF AND BROCCOLI STIR-FRY

Cooking Time: 15 minutes Servings: 4

Ingredients:
- 400g (14 oz) beef sirloin, thinly sliced
- 1 broccoli head, cut into florets
- 1 red bell pepper, sliced
- 2 cloves garlic, minced
- 2 tablespoons soy sauce
- 1 tablespoon oyster sauce
- 1 tablespoon olive oil
- 1 teaspoon ginger, grated
- Cooked rice for serving

Instructions:

1. Preheat your air fryer to 180°C (356°F) for 5 minutes.
2. In a large bowl, toss the thinly sliced beef with soy sauce and grated ginger. Allow it to marinate for a few minutes.
3. Place the marinated beef in the air fryer basket and air fry for 5-7 minutes until cooked to your preference. Remove and set aside.
4. In the same bowl, toss the broccoli florets and red bell pepper with olive oil.
5. Place the mixed vegetables in the air fryer basket and air fry for 7-10 minutes until tender.
6. While the vegetables are cooking, heat a skillet over medium heat and sauté the minced garlic.
7. Add the cooked beef to the skillet, along with oyster sauce. Cook for a few minutes to combine.
8. Serve the beef and broccoli stir-fry over cooked rice.

Nutrition Information (per serving, without rice):
- Calories: 280
- Protein: 25g
- Carbohydrates: 12g
- Fat: 15g
- Fiber: 5g

RECIPE 15: LEMON DRIZZLE CAKE

Cooking Time: 25 minutes Servings: 8

Ingredients:
- 200g (7.1 oz) self-raising flour
- 200g (7.1 oz) unsalted butter, softened
- 200g (7.1 oz) caster sugar
- 4 large eggs
- Zest and juice of 2 lemons
- 100g (3.5 oz) icing sugar

Instructions:
1. Preheat your air fryer to 180°C (356°F) for 5 minutes.
2. In a bowl, beat together the softened butter and caster sugar until light and fluffy.
3. Gradually add the eggs, one at a time, mixing well after each addition.
4. Fold in the self-raising flour and the zest of 2 lemons.
5. Grease and line a cake tin that fits inside your air fryer basket.
6. Pour the cake batter into the tin and smooth the top.
7. Place the tin in the air fryer basket.
8. Air fry for 20-25 minutes until a skewer comes out clean when inserted into the cake.
9. While the cake is cooking, mix the lemon juice and icing sugar to make a drizzle.
10. Once the cake is cooked, drizzle the lemon icing over the top.

Nutrition Information (per serving):
- Calories: 400
- Protein: 5g
- Carbohydrates: 45g
- Fat: 20g
- Fiber: 1g

Chapter 9: Desserts and Sweets

Indulge your sweet tooth with delightful desserts and sweets prepared in your air fryer. Each dessert recipe includes cooking time, servings, ingredients, instructions, and nutritional information in UK measurements.

Recipe 1: Air-Fried Apple Pie

Cooking Time: 15 minutes Servings: 4

Ingredients:
- 2 sheets of puff pastry, thawed
- 2 medium apples, peeled, cored, and diced
- 50g (1.8 oz) granulated sugar
- 1/2 teaspoon ground cinnamon
- 1/4 teaspoon ground nutmeg
- 1 egg, beaten
- Icing sugar for dusting

Instructions:
1. Preheat your air fryer to 180°C (356°F) for 5 minutes.
2. In a bowl, combine the diced apples, granulated sugar, ground cinnamon, and ground nutmeg.
3. Cut the puff pastry sheets into squares or rectangles.
4. Place a portion of the apple mixture in the centre of each pastry square.
5. Fold the pastry over the apples to form a triangle or rectangle, then crimp the edges with a fork to seal.
6. Brush the pastry with beaten egg.
7. Place the apple pies in the air fryer basket.
8. Air fry for 12-15 minutes until the pies are golden and the apples are tender.
9. Dust with icing sugar before serving.

Nutrition Information (per serving):
- Calories: 280
- Protein: 4g
- Carbohydrates: 40g
- Fat: 12g
- Fiber: 2g

Recipe 2: Mini Chocolate Lava Cakes

Cooking Time: 10 minutes Servings: 4

Ingredients:
- 100g (3.5 oz) dark chocolate, chopped
- 100g (3.5 oz) unsalted butter
- 2 large eggs
- 50g (1.8 oz) granulated sugar
- 40g (1.4 oz) plain flour
- 1/2 teaspoon vanilla extract
- Icing sugar for dusting

Instructions:
1. Preheat your air fryer to 180°C (356°F) for 5 minutes.
2. In a microwave-safe bowl, melt the dark chocolate and unsalted butter together, stirring until smooth.

3. In a separate bowl, whisk the eggs and granulated sugar until well combined.
4. Gradually fold the melted chocolate mixture into the egg mixture.
5. Stir in the plain flour and vanilla extract.
6. Grease and flour small ramekins or baking dishes.
7. Pour the chocolate batter into the prepared ramekins.
8. Place the ramekins in the air fryer basket.
9. Air fry for 8-10 minutes until the cakes are set around the edges but still slightly gooey in the centre.
10. Dust with icing sugar before serving. Careful, the centres will be hot!

Nutrition Information (per serving):
- Calories: 350
- Protein: 5g
- Carbohydrates: 25g
- Fat: 25g
- Fiber: 2g

RECIPE 3: CINNAMON SUGAR DONUTS

Cooking Time: 8 minutes Servings: 4

Ingredients:
- 200g (7.1 oz) plain flour
- 150ml (5.3 fl oz) whole milk
- 50g (1.8 oz) granulated sugar
- 2 teaspoons baking powder
- 1/2 teaspoon ground cinnamon
- 1/4 teaspoon salt
- 1 large egg
- 1 teaspoon vanilla extract
- 2 tablespoons unsalted butter, melted
- For the cinnamon sugar coating: 50g (1.8 oz) granulated sugar and 1 teaspoon ground cinnamon

Instructions:
1. Preheat your air fryer to 180°C (356°F) for 5 minutes.
2. In a bowl, whisk together the plain flour, granulated sugar, baking powder, ground cinnamon, and salt.
3. In a separate bowl, combine the whole milk, egg, vanilla extract, and melted unsalted butter.
4. Gradually add the wet mixture to the dry mixture, stirring until just combined.
5. Spoon the donut batter into a donut pan, filling each cavity about two-thirds full.
6. Place the donut pan in the air fryer basket.
7. Air fry for 6-8 minutes until the donuts are golden brown and cooked through.
8. While the donuts are still warm, toss them in the cinnamon sugar coating.

Nutrition Information (per serving):
- Calories: 300
- Protein: 6g
- Carbohydrates: 50g
- Fat: 8g
- Fiber: 2g

RECIPE 4: BERRY-STUFFED FRENCH TOAST

Cooking Time: 15 minutes Servings: 4

Ingredients:
- 8 slices of thick bread
- 4 large eggs
- 200ml (7 fl oz) whole milk
- 50g (1.8 oz) granulated sugar

- 1 teaspoon ground cinnamon
- 1 teaspoon vanilla extract
- 150g (5.3 oz) mixed berries (e.g., strawberries, blueberries, raspberries)
- Maple syrup for serving

Instructions:
1. Preheat your air fryer to 180°C (356°F) for 5 minutes.
2. In a bowl, whisk together the eggs, whole milk, granulated sugar, ground cinnamon, and vanilla extract.
3. Spread the mixed berries on half of the bread slices.
4. Top with the remaining bread slices to make sandwiches.
5. Dip each sandwich into the egg mixture, ensuring it's well-coated.
6. Place the stuffed French toast sandwiches in the air fryer basket.
7. Air fry for 12-15 minutes until the French toast is golden and cooked through.
8. Serve with maple syrup.

Nutrition Information (per serving, without maple syrup):
- Calories: 300
- Protein: 10g
- Carbohydrates: 40g
- Fat: 10g
- Fiber: 4g

RECIPE 5: CHICKEN AND MUSHROOM PIE

Cooking Time: 15 minutes Servings: 4

Ingredients:
- 4 boneless, skinless chicken breasts
- 200g (7.1 oz) mushrooms, sliced
- 1 onion, chopped
- 2 cloves garlic, minced
- 200ml (7 FL oz) double cream
- 1 tablespoon olive oil
- 1 teaspoon dried thyme
- Salt and black pepper to taste
- Puff pastry sheets for topping
- 1 egg, beaten (for egg wash)

Instructions:
1. Preheat your air fryer to 180°C (356°F) for 5 minutes.
2. In a skillet, heat the olive oil over medium heat. Sauté the chopped onion and minced garlic until translucent.
3. Add the sliced mushrooms and cook until they release their moisture.
4. Cut the chicken breasts into bite-sized pieces and add them to the skillet. Cook until the chicken is no longer pink.
5. Stir in the double cream, dried thyme, salt, and black pepper. Simmer for a few minutes.
6. Pour the chicken and mushroom mixture into an oven-safe dish.
7. Top with puff pastry and brush with beaten egg for a golden finish.
8. Place the dish in the air fryer basket.
9. Air fry for 12-15 minutes until the pastry is puffed and golden.
10. Serve this hearty pie as a comforting main course.

Nutrition Information (per serving):
- Calories: 450
- Protein: 25g
- Carbohydrates: 20g
- Fat: 28g
- Fiber: 2g

RECIPE 6: ROASTED VEGETABLES AND HALLOUMI

Cooking Time: 12 minutes Servings: 4

Ingredients:
- 200g (7.1 oz) halloumi cheese, sliced
- 2 red bell peppers, cut into chunks
- 2 courgettes (zucchinis), sliced
- 1 red onion, sliced
- 2 cloves garlic, minced
- 2 tablespoons olive oil
- 1 teaspoon dried oregano
- Salt and black pepper to taste
- Fresh basil leaves for garnish

Instructions:
1. Preheat your air fryer to 200°C (392°F) for 5 minutes.
2. In a large bowl, toss the halloumi slices, red bell peppers, courgettes, and red onion with olive oil and minced garlic.
3. Season with dried oregano, salt, and black pepper.
4. Place the coated vegetables and halloumi in the air fryer basket.
5. Air fry for 10-12 minutes until the vegetables are tender and the halloumi is golden.
6. Garnish with fresh basil leaves before serving.

Nutrition Information (per serving):
- Calories: 280
- Protein: 15g
- Carbohydrates: 10g
- Fat: 20g
- Fiber: 3g

RECIPE 7: PRAWN AND AVOCADO SALAD

Cooking Time: 5 minutes Servings: 4

Ingredients:
- 300g (10.6 oz) cooked prawns
- 2 avocados, diced
- 1 cucumber, diced
- 1 red chili, finely chopped (adjust to taste)
- 1 lime, juiced
- Fresh coriander leaves for garnish
- Salt and black pepper to taste

Instructions:
1. In a bowl, combine the cooked prawns, diced avocados, diced cucumber, and finely chopped red chili.
2. Drizzle with lime juice and season with salt and black pepper.
3. Gently toss to combine all the ingredients.
4. Preheat your air fryer to 180°C (356°F) for 5 minutes.
5. Divide the prawn and avocado salad among serving plates.
6. Garnish with fresh coriander leaves.
7. This light and refreshing salad make for a perfect appetizer or light lunch.

Nutrition Information (per serving):
- Calories: 200
- Protein: 15g
- Carbohydrates: 10g
- Fat: 12g
- Fiber: 6g

RECIPE 8: BEEF AND MUSHROOM SKEWERS

Cooking Time: 10 minutes Servings: 4

Ingredients:
- 400g (14 oz) beef sirloin, cut into cubes
- 200g (7.1 oz) mushrooms
- 1 red onion, cut into chunks
- 2 cloves garlic, minced
- 2 tablespoons olive oil
- 1 teaspoon dried rosemary
- Salt and black pepper to taste

Instructions:
1. Preheat your air fryer to 200°C (392°F) for 5 minutes.
2. In a bowl, combine the beef cubes, mushrooms, red onion, and minced garlic.
3. Toss with olive oil, dried rosemary, salt, and black pepper.
4. Thread the beef, mushrooms, and onion onto skewers.
5. Place the skewers in the air fryer basket.
6. Air fry for 8-10 minutes until the beef is cooked to your preference.
7. Serve these flavourful skewers as a main course or appetizer.

Nutrition Information (per serving):
- Calories: 300
- Protein: 25g
- Carbohydrates: 6g
- Fat: 20g
- Fiber: 2g

RECIPE 9: BAKED POTATOES WITH SOUR CREAM AND CHIVES

Cooking Time: 40 minutes Servings: 4

Ingredients:
- 4 large potatoes
- 100ml (3.4 fl oz) sour cream
- Fresh chives, chopped
- Salt and black pepper to taste

Instructions:
1. Preheat your air fryer to 200°C (392°F) for 5 minutes.
2. Pierce the potatoes with a fork a few times to allow steam to escape.
3. Place the potatoes directly in the air fryer basket.
4. Air fry for 35-40 minutes, turning them halfway through, until the potatoes are tender and the skin is crispy.
5. Cut a slit in the top of each potato and fluff the insides with a fork.
6. Top with sour cream and chopped chives.
7. Season with salt and black pepper to taste.

Nutrition Information (per serving):
- Calories: 250
- Protein: 5g
- Carbohydrates: 50g
- Fat: 3g
- Fiber: 5g

RECIPE 10: PAKORAS (VEGETABLE FRITTERS)

Cooking Time: 10 minutes Servings: 4

Ingredients:
- 200g (7.1 oz) chickpea flour (gram flour)
- 1 teaspoon ground cumin
- 1/2 teaspoon ground coriander
- 1/2 teaspoon turmeric
- 1/2 teaspoon chili powder (adjust to taste)
- 1 teaspoon garam masala
- 1/2 teaspoon baking powder
- Salt to taste
- 200ml (7 fl oz) water
- 200g (7.1 oz) mixed vegetables (e.g., onions, spinach, potatoes), finely chopped
- Cooking oil for greasing

Instructions:
1. Preheat your air fryer to 200°C (392°F) for 5 minutes.
2. In a bowl, combine the chickpea flour, ground cumin, ground coriander, turmeric, chili powder, garam masala, baking powder, and salt.
3. Gradually add water to the dry ingredients to make a smooth batter.
4. Stir in the finely chopped mixed vegetables to the batter.
5. Grease the air fryer basket with cooking oil.
6. Drop spoonsful of the batter into the basket to make small pakora fritters, leaving space between them.
7. Air fry for 8-10 minutes until the pakoras are crispy and golden.
8. Serve with chutney or yogurt sauce.

Nutrition Information (per serving, without chutney or sauce):
- Calories: 150
- Protein: 4g
- Carbohydrates: 25g
- Fat: 3g
- Fiber: 5g

RECIPE 11: STUFFED CHICKEN BREASTS

Cooking Time: 18 minutes Servings: 4

Ingredients:
- 4 boneless, skinless chicken breasts
- 200g (7.1 oz) mushrooms, finely chopped
- 1 small onion, finely chopped
- 2 cloves garlic, minced
- 50g (1.8 oz) grated Cheddar cheese
- 1 tablespoon olive oil
- 1 teaspoon dried thyme
- 1 teaspoon dried rosemary
- Salt and black pepper to taste

Instructions:
1. Preheat your air fryer to 180°C (356°F) for 5 minutes.
2. In a skillet, heat the olive oil over medium heat. Sauté the chopped onion and minced garlic until translucent. Add the chopped mushrooms and cook until they release their moisture.
3. Stir in the dried thyme, dried rosemary, salt, and black pepper. Remove from heat and allow the mixture to cool.
4. Cut a pocket into each chicken breast and stuff them with the mushroom mixture and grated Cheddar cheese.

5. Place the stuffed chicken breasts in the air fryer basket.
6. Air fry for 16-18 minutes until the chicken is cooked through and the cheese is melted and bubbly.

Nutrition Information (per serving):
- Calories: 250
- Protein: 30g
- Carbohydrates: 5g
- Fat: 12g
- Fiber: 2g

RECIPE 12: CREAMY PESTO PASTA

Cooking Time: 10 minutes Servings: 4

Ingredients:
- 300g (10.6 oz) penne pasta
- 200ml (7 fl oz) double cream
- 3 tablespoons pesto sauce
- 50g (1.8 oz) grated Parmesan cheese
- Salt and black pepper to taste
- Fresh basil leaves for garnish

Instructions:
1. Cook the penne pasta according to the package instructions until al dente. Drain and set aside.
2. In a saucepan, heat the double cream and pesto sauce over low heat, stirring until well combined.
3. Stir in the grated Parmesan cheese and season with salt and black pepper.
4. Pour the creamy pesto sauce over the cooked pasta and toss to coat.
5. Preheat your air fryer to 180°C (356°F) for 5 minutes.
6. Place the pasta in an oven-safe dish and air fry for 8-10 minutes until the top is golden and bubbling.
7. Garnish with fresh basil leaves before serving.

Nutrition Information (per serving):
- Calories: 450
- Protein: 12g
- Carbohydrates: 40g
- Fat: 25g
- Fiber: 2g

RECIPE 13: VEGETARIAN SPRING ROLLS

Cooking Time: 10 minutes Servings: 4

Ingredients:
- 8 spring roll wrappers
- 200g (7.1 oz) bean sprouts
- 1 carrot, julienned
- 1 courgette (zucchini), julienned
- 100g (3.5 oz) rice vermicelli noodles, cooked
- 2 cloves garlic, minced
- 2 tablespoons soy sauce
- 1 tablespoon olive oil
- Sweet chili sauce for dipping

Instructions:
1. Preheat your air fryer to 180°C (356°F) for 5 minutes.
2. In a skillet, heat the olive oil over medium heat. Sauté the minced garlic until fragrant.
3. Add the bean sprouts, julienned carrot, and julienned courgette. Sauté until the vegetables are tender.

4. Stir in the cooked rice vermicelli noodles and soy sauce. Cook for an additional 2 minutes.
5. Place a spring roll wrapper on a clean surface, then add a portion of the vegetable and noodle mixture.
6. Fold the sides of the wrapper in, then roll up tightly.
7. Place the vegetarian spring rolls in the air fryer basket.
8. Air fry for 8-10 minutes until the spring rolls are crispy and golden.
9. Serve with sweet chili sauce for dipping.

Nutrition Information (per serving, without sauce):
- Calories: 180
- Protein: 4g
- Carbohydrates: 30g
- Fat: 4g
- Fiber: 3g

RECIPE 14: BEEF AND BROCCOLI STIR-FRY

Cooking Time: 15 minutes Servings: 4

Ingredients:
- 400g (14 oz) beef sirloin, thinly sliced
- 1 broccoli head, cut into florets
- 1 red bell pepper, sliced
- 2 cloves garlic, minced
- 2 tablespoons soy sauce
- 1 tablespoon oyster sauce
- 1 teaspoon sesame oil
- 1 tablespoon corn-starch
- 2 tablespoons water
- Cooking oil for stir-frying
- Cooked rice for serving

Instructions:
1. In a bowl, whisk together the soy sauce, oyster sauce, sesame oil, corn-starch, and water. Set aside.
2. Preheat your air fryer to 180°C (356°F) for 5 minutes.
3. In a wok or skillet, heat cooking oil over high heat. Stir-fry the thinly sliced beef until browned. Remove from the wok and set aside.
4. In the same wok, add more oil if needed, then stir-fry the minced garlic, red bell pepper slices, and broccoli florets until tender.
5. Return the cooked beef to the wok.
6. Pour the sauce mixture over the stir-fry and cook until the sauce thickens.
7. Preheat your air fryer to 180°C (356°F) for 5 minutes.
8. Place the beef and broccoli stir-fry in an oven-safe dish and air fry for 8-10 minutes until heated through.
9. Serve with cooked rice.

Nutrition Information (per serving, without rice):
- Calories: 250
- Protein: 20g
- Carbohydrates: 10g
- Fat: 15g
- Fiber: 4g

RECIPE 15: LEMON DRIZZLE CAKE

Cooking Time: 25 minutes Servings: 8

Ingredients:

- 200g (7.1 oz) unsalted butter
- 200g (7.1 oz) granulated sugar
- 4 large eggs
- 200g (7.1 oz) self-rising flour
- Zest and juice of 2 lemons
- 100g (3.5 oz) icing sugar

Instructions:
1. In a bowl, beat the unsalted butter and granulated sugar until light and fluffy.
2. Gradually add the large eggs, one at a time, mixing well after each addition.
3. Fold in the self-raising flour and the zest of 2 lemons.
4. Grease and line a cake tin that fits inside your air fryer basket.
5. Pour the cake batter into the tin and smooth the top.
6. Place the tin in the air fryer basket.
7. Air fry for 20-25 minutes until a skewer comes out clean when inserted into the cake.
8. While the cake is cooking, mix the lemon juice and icing sugar to make a drizzle.
9. Once the cake is cooked, drizzle the lemon icing over the top.

Nutrition Information (per serving):
- Calories: 400
- Protein: 5g
- Carbohydrates: 45g
- Fat: 20g
- Fiber: 1g

RECIPE 16: BAKED BRIE WITH CRANBERRY SAUCE

Cooking Time: 10 minutes Servings: 4

Ingredients:
- 1 wheel of Brie cheese
- 1/2 cup cranberry sauce
- 2 tablespoons honey
- A handful of fresh cranberries
- Fresh rosemary sprigs
- Baguette slices for serving

Instructions:
1. Preheat your air fryer to 180°C (356°F) for 5 minutes.
2. Place the wheel of Brie in a heatproof dish.
3. Top the Brie with cranberry sauce and drizzle honey over it.
4. Add fresh cranberries and a few rosemary sprigs for flavor.
5. Place the dish in the air fryer basket.
6. Air fry for 8-10 minutes until the Brie is soft and gooey.
7. Serve with baguette slices for dipping.

Nutrition Information (per serving, not including baguette):
- Calories: 220
- Protein: 7g
- Carbohydrates: 20g
- Fat: 12g
- Fiber: 1g

CHAPTER 10: CUSTOMIZING YOUR RECIPES

SPICE BLENDS AND SEASONINGS

One of the joys of cooking with an air fryer is the ability to experiment with different spice blends and seasonings to enhance the flavour of your dishes. Here are some popular spice blends and seasonings you can use in your air fryer recipes:

1. All-Purpose Seasoning:
A versatile blend of salt, pepper, garlic powder, onion powder, and paprika. It works well on meats, vegetables, and even popcorn.

2. Italian Seasoning:
A mix of dried herbs like basil, oregano, thyme, and rosemary. Perfect for adding an Italian twist to your dishes.

3. Cajun Seasoning:
A fiery blend of paprika, cayenne pepper, garlic powder, and various herbs. Ideal for giving your meals a spicy kick.

4. Curry Powder:
A combination of ground spices like turmeric, coriander, cumin, and cardamom. Great for Indian-inspired recipes.

5. Lemon Pepper Seasoning:
Zesty and tangy with a mixture of lemon zest and black pepper. Adds brightness to chicken, seafood, and vegetables.

6. BBQ Rub:
A smoky and sweet blend featuring ingredients like brown sugar, paprika, and cayenne. Perfect for grilling and roasting.

7. Herbes de Provence:
A fragrant mix of dried herbs like lavender, marjoram, and thyme. Adds a touch of French flair to your dishes.

Feel free to create your own custom spice blends to suit your taste preferences. Remember to store them in airtight containers to maintain their freshness.

SAUCES AND DIPS

Sauces and dips can take your air fryer recipes to the next level. Here are some popular options and suggestions for using them:

1. Tomato-Based Sauces:
Classic tomato sauce, marinara, and salsa are great for topping chicken, seafood, and vegetables. Sprinkle with cheese for added richness.

2. Homemade Mayonnaise:

Create your own mayonnaise with egg yolks, mustard, and oil. Use it as a dip for potato wedges or a creamy dressing for salads.

3. Garlic Aioli:
Blend mayonnaise with minced garlic, lemon juice, and salt. It's perfect for dipping crispy snacks like mozzarella sticks.

4. Teriyaki Sauce:
A sweet and savoury sauce made from soy sauce, sugar, and ginger. Glaze your air-fried chicken wings with it for an Asian twist.

5. Pesto:
Basil, pine nuts, Parmesan cheese, and olive oil make a delightful pesto. Drizzle it over roasted vegetables or use it as a pasta sauce.

6. Honey Mustard:
Mix honey, Dijon mustard, and a splash of vinegar for a sweet and tangy dip. It pairs wonderfully with air-fried chicken tenders.

7. Guacamole:
Avocado, lime, tomato, and cilantro combine to create a creamy dip. Serve it alongside air-fried vegetable spring rolls.

8. Tzatziki:
Greek yogurt, cucumber, dill, and garlic make a refreshing dip. Perfect for pairing with air-fried meatballs.

Experiment with different sauces and dips to discover exciting new flavour combinations. Don't be afraid to adjust the ingredients to suit your taste.

RECIPE MODIFICATIONS
Customizing recipes to meet your dietary preferences or restrictions is easy with an air fryer. Here are some common modifications you can make:

1. Vegetarian and Vegan Variations:
Substitute meat with plant-based options like tofu, tempeh, or seitan. Use vegetable broth instead of meat-based broths in soups and stews.

2. Gluten-Free Adaptations:
Replace wheat-based ingredients with gluten-free alternatives, such as almond flour, rice flour, or gluten-free breadcrumbs.

3. Low-Sodium Options:
Reduce salt in your recipes and use herbs, spices, and citrus zest to enhance flavour.

4. Low-Fat Cooking:
Use an oil sprayer to apply a minimal amount of oil to your ingredients, or cook without oil for a healthier option.

5. Portion Control:
Adjust the quantity of ingredients to match the number of servings you need. Air fryers are versatile and can accommodate various portion sizes.

6. Dietary Restrictions:
If you have specific dietary restrictions (e.g., keto, paleo), research and select recipes that align with your dietary goals.

Remember to keep a notebook of your modifications and the results, so you can replicate successful adaptations in the future. With your air fryer and a little creativity, you can tailor your recipes to suit your personal tastes and dietary needs. Enjoy the endless possibilities

CHAPTER 11: TROUBLESHOOTING AND FAQ

COMMON AIR FRYER PROBLEMS

Air fryers are generally reliable, but you might encounter a few issues along the way. Here are some common problems and their solutions:

1. Food Isn't Crispy:
Solution: Ensure your air fryer is preheated, and don't overcrowd the basket. Shake or flip the food halfway through cooking. Lightly coat food with oil or cooking spray.

2. Uneven Cooking:
Solution: Arrange food evenly in a single layer. Some air fryers may require rotating the basket or tray during cooking.

3. Smoke or Odor:
Solution: Check for excess oil or food debris in the bottom tray. Clean your air fryer regularly to prevent smoking.

4. Food Sticking to Basket:
Solution: Use a non-stick cooking spray or parchment paper to prevent sticking. Be cautious when using marinades or sauces that can stick.

5. Overcooking or Burning:
Solution: Adjust cooking time and temperature as needed. Start with lower settings and increase if necessary.

6. Air Fryer Not Heating:
Solution: Check the power source and ensure the air fryer is properly plugged in. If the heating element is malfunctioning, contact customer support.

7. Unpleasant Smells:
Solution: Regularly clean the air fryer, especially the basket and tray, to prevent odors from accumulating.

8. Loud Noise:
Solution: Some air fryers can be noisy during operation, but unusual or excessive noise may indicate a mechanical issue. Contact customer support if needed.

9. Condensation on Food:
Solution: Pat dry food with paper towels before air frying to reduce condensation. Also, consider using a higher temperature.

ANSWERS TO FREQUENTLY ASKED QUESTIONS

Q1: What is an air fryer, and how does it work?
A1: An air fryer is a kitchen appliance that cooks by circulating hot air around the food. It uses convection to produce a crispy, fried-like texture without the need for excessive oil.

Q2: Can I cook frozen food in an air fryer?
A2: Yes, you can cook frozen food in an air fryer. Adjust the cooking time and temperature to accommodate frozen items.

Q3: Do I need to preheat my air fryer?
A3: Preheating is recommended for most recipes. It helps ensure even cooking and a crispy texture.

Q4: Is it safe to use oil in an air fryer?
A4: Yes, you can use a small amount of oil or cooking spray to enhance the texture and flavour of your dishes. Be cautious not to overuse oil, as it may cause smoking.

Q5: Can I open the air fryer during cooking to check on the food?
A5: You can open the air fryer to check on the food, but doing so may affect cooking time and temperature. It's best to check towards the end of the cooking cycle.

Q6: How do I clean my air fryer?
A6: Unplug the air fryer and allow it to cool. Remove the basket and tray and wash them with warm, soapy water. Wipe down the interior and exterior of the air fryer with a damp cloth. Refer to your user manual for specific cleaning instructions.

Q7: Can I use aluminium foil or parchment paper in my air fryer?
A7: Yes, you can use aluminium foil or parchment paper to line the basket or tray to prevent sticking or make clean-up easier. Just make sure it doesn't block the airflow.

Q8: What types of food can I cook in an air fryer?
A8: You can cook a wide variety of foods in an air fryer, including vegetables, meats, seafood, poultry, and even desserts.

Q9: Is an air fryer a healthier cooking option compared to deep frying?
A9: Air frying typically requires less oil than deep frying, making it a healthier choice. However, the overall healthiness of the meal depends on the ingredients and cooking methods used.

CONCLUSION

In this air fryer cookbook for beginners, you've explored the benefits of cooking with an air fryer, learned essential cooking techniques, discovered safety tips, and enjoyed a wide range of recipes designed for a UK audience. Whether you're a novice in the kitchen or a seasoned cook, the air fryer offers a convenient and healthy way to prepare delicious meals.

Remember to experiment, customize, and enjoy the culinary journey as you create tasty dishes with your air fryer. Happy cooking!

RECAP AND FINAL TIPS

- Congratulations on completing this air fryer cookbook! Here's a quick recap of what you've learned and some final tips to enhance your air frying experience:
- You've learned about the benefits of cooking with an air fryer, from healthier meals to quicker cooking times.
- Essential cooking techniques, such as preheating, temperature and timing, flipping and shaking, and using oil or cooking spray, are now at your fingertips.
- Safety guidelines have equipped you with the knowledge to use your air fryer responsibly and securely.
- You've explored a wide array of recipes, from appetizers to main courses and desserts, all tailored to the UK audience.

FINAL TIPS:

Experiment and Customize: Don't be afraid to get creative with your air fryer recipes. Try different seasonings, sauces, and ingredients to create your signature dishes.

Keep It Clean: Regularly clean your air fryer to prevent odors, maintain its performance, and extend its lifespan. Refer to your user manual for specific cleaning instructions.

Preheating Matters: Preheating your air fryer ensures consistent and even cooking. It's an essential step for most recipes.

Don't Overcrowd: Overcrowding the air fryer basket can lead to uneven cooking. Ensure there's enough space between items for the hot air to circulate.

Use Accessories: Explore compatible air fryer accessories like racks, skewers, and silicone melds to expand your cooking possibilities.

Keep an Eye on Cooking Time: As you get familiar with your air fryer, adjust cooking times to match your preferences and the size of the ingredients.

Practice Makes Perfect: Like any cooking method, practice is key to mastering your air fryer. Don't be discouraged if your first attempts aren't flawless.

DISCOVERING YOUR CULINARY STYLE WITH THE AIR FRYER

Your air fryer is a versatile kitchen companion that can help you discover your culinary style. Whether you're a health-conscious cook, a comfort food enthusiast, or an experimental chef, the air fryer provides endless possibilities. Embrace your creativity and try new recipes, flavours, and techniques to develop your unique cooking style.

APPENDIX: CONVERSION CHARTS

Here are some handy conversion charts to assist you in the kitchen:

- Temperature Conversion Chart
- Fahrenheit (°F) to Celsius (°C):
- To convert Fahrenheit to Celsius, subtract 32, then multiply by 5/9.
- Example: 350°F = (350 - 32) × 5/9 ≈ 176.67°C.
- Celsius (°C) to Fahrenheit (°F):
- To convert Celsius to Fahrenheit, multiply by 9/5, then add 32.
- Example: 200°C = (200 × 9/5) + 32 ≈ 392°F.
- Volume and Weight Conversions
- Fluid Ounces (FL oz) to Millilitres (ml):
- 1 FL oz = 29.5735 ml.
- Cups to Millilitres (ml):
- 1 cup = 236.59 ml.
- Ounces (oz) to Grams (g):
- 1 oz = 28.3495 g.
- Pounds (lb) to Kilograms (kg):
- 1 lb = 0.453592 kg.

These conversion charts can help you adapt recipes and measurements to fit your preferences and the equipment you have available.

Enjoy your air frying adventures, and don't hesitate to explore, innovate, and make each meal your own. Happy cooking!

Printed in Great Britain
by Amazon

46286523R00044